NTC's Dictionary of THEATRE and DRAMA TERMS

NTC's Dictionary of THEATRE and DRAMA TERMS

Jonnie Patricia Mobley, Ph.D.
Drama Department
Cuesta College
San Luis Obispo, California

NTC Publishing Group
NTC/Contemporary Publishing Company

Library of Congress Cataloging-in-Publication Data
is available from the United States Library of Congress.

Published by NTC Publishing Group
An imprint of NTC/Contemporary Publishing Company
4255 West Touhy Avenue, Lincolnwood (Chicago), Illinois 60646-1975 U.S.A.

Printed in the United States of America
International Standard Book Number: 0-8442-5333-2
18 17 16 15 14 13 12 11 10 9 8 7 6 5 4 3 2

Preface

The theatre is so rich in tradition, so fascinating in conventions and language, that the pleasure and enchantment of a performance, for audience and actors alike, can only be enhanced by knowing why things are done as they are and why they are called what they are.

Think for a moment of words and phrases, whose origin is the theatre, that have found their way into everyday speech:

Tom's a sugar-cured ham.
You're in the spotlight now.
Dad's playing the heavy again.
That's your cue to say something.
Fred's always there, waiting in the wings.
Maria is forever playing the ingenue.

To these, you can probably add dozens more, expressions that add spice and sparkle to conversation. Indeed, we often find ourselves agreeing with Shakespeare that "all the world's a stage."

Of necessity, the entries in this book are brief. But each should serve to explain the meaning of a term and, I hope, to whet the reader's appetite for the plays cited as examples, to read these and see them performed.

Because it is frustrating to look up a term and be directed elsewhere, every entry in this dictionary provides some information, even when a term is better known by another name. References to supplemental information are listed following the entry. This is not to imply that casual browsing in this book is discouraged. On the contrary, serendipity is one of the sustaining joys of the theatre.

This book is dedicated to my husband Dwight, whose encouragement and technical assistance were invaluable, and to Sister Laurentia Digges, CSJ, and Sister St. George Skurla, CSJ, whose vocabulary lists in those long-ago literature courses sparked my interest and eventually led to this book.

abstract set. Uses drapes, free-standing doors, and window frames to convey the idea of a setting without any actual set construction.
See ARRAS SETTING, CURTAIN SET, CYCLORAMA, MINIMAL SETTING.

absurd, theatre of the. A convention defined by contemporary critic Martin Esslin as "striving to express its sense of the senselessness of the human condition and the inadequacy of the rational approach by the open abandonment of rational devices and discursive thought." Plays in the absurdist tradition attempt to show the irrational and illogical aspects of life through absurd characters, dialogue, and situations. The plays of N. F. Simpson, Harold Pinter, and Edward Albee fall within this category, but the form has been most popular in France because of its ties to existentialism and can be seen in the plays of Jean Genet, Eugène Ionesco, and Samuel Beckett. In Beckett's *Waiting for Godot,* two tramps wait interminably and in great uncertainty for someone who never arrives, who may not have specified this meeting place, and who may never have promised to appear at all.
See ANTIHERO, CONVENTION, DADAISM, EXISTENTIALISM.

academic theatre. Theatre connected with school and having educational, rather than commercial, goals. The physical plant may be anything from a classroom or outdoor platform to a full-size proscenium arch theatre. The actors are usually drawn from theatre classes, although there may be guest performances from community members or by a professional artist-in-residence. The works produced may be well-known standards of the commercial theatre or student-written works-in-progress.

See AMERICAN COLLEGE THEATRE FESTIVAL, COLLABORATIVE THEATRE, EDUCATIONAL THEATRE, WORKSHOP PRODUCTION.

act. A major division of a play. Acts may be further divided into scenes. Either may be used to indicate a change of time or place. In classical drama, plays were performed without interruption, but divisions, such as *epode*, are indicated in present-day texts. In print, Elizabethan plays are usually divided by editors into five acts, although no such divisions are made in early manuscripts. Until recently, the three-act structure was popular, but more and more plays are being divided into two acts.

See CURTAIN LINE, SCENE.

act drop. A painted cloth lowered to close the proscenium opening between acts.

acting area. The space, be it stage, platform, or floor, set aside for performing the play.

See APRON, BOARDS, DECK, EKKYKLEMA, FORESTAGE, HOT SPOT, STAGE.

action. The movement in the play from the initial entanglement, through rising action, climax, and falling action to resolution.

See ANAGNORISIS, ANTICLIMAX, CLIMAX, COMPLICATION, CONFLICT, CRISIS, DENOUEMENT, EXPOSITION, FALLING ACTION, MOVEMENT, RECOGNITION SCENE, REVERSAL, RISING ACTION, TURNING POINT.

actor. One who performs a role or represents a character in a play. The term is now used for both men and women performers.

See CAST, CASTING, CREATE A ROLE, ECONOMY OF ROLES, ENSEMBLE PLAYING, GEORGE SPELVIN, HAM, HYPOKRITES, STAR TURN, THESPIS, TYPECASTING, UNDERSTUDY.

actor proof. A play or sketch that is almost impervious to bad acting. Francis Swann's *Out of the Frying Pan,* a hit on Broadway in the 1940s and a staple of community and academic theatre ever since, has such ingratiating characters, such a tightly constructed plot, and so much fun and goodwill built into it that it can survive the most amateurish production.

Actors' Equity. The professional stage actors' association in the United States that regulates actors' salaries, working conditions, and terms of employment. British Actors' Equity includes film, radio, and television actors in its membership. In California an equity actor may, with permission, work with non-equity personnel in an "equity-waiver" production.

See EQUITY WAIVER HOUSE.

Actors' Studio. Acting workshop founded in New York City in the 1940s. Lee Strasberg was the artistic director for many years and under his leadership the studio became famous for its techniques of preparation and performance that came to be called *method acting.* Famous alumni include Marlon Brando, Geraldine Page, Shirley Knight, and Kim Stanley.

See AFFECTIVE MEMORY, EMOTIONAL RECALL, METHOD ACTING, MOTIVATION, SENSE MEMORY.

actress. A woman or girl who represents a character. The term *actor* is now used for performers of both sexes.

See ACTOR.

act tunes. Musical interludes between acts. Originally composed for a particular production and played by live musicians, act tunes are now more often taped music chosen to sustain the mood of the play.

See ENTR'ACTE, OLIO, INTERLUDE.

ad-lib. To improvise something—dialog, stage business—not given specifically in the script. Ad-libbing is often unrehearsed and done in response to an emergency, such as actors forgetting their lines, or props and scenery breaking. In addition, the playwright may merely indicate general business, such as "crowd ad-libs amazement," and appropriate lines are decided on in rehearsal and kept through the run of the play.

See FLUFFED LINE, IMPROVISATION, THEATRE GAMES.

aesthetic distance. A physical or psychological separation between the audience and the action of a play. Such separation is necessary to maintain the artistic illusion of the performance. Participatory theatre attempts to eliminate this distance.

See ALIENATION EFFECT, FOURTH WALL, PARTICIPATORY THEATRE, PRESENTATIONAL, SUSPENSION OF DISBELIEF.

aesthetics. The branch of philosophy that studies the arts and, especially, the principles of beauty.

See CRITICISM.

affective memory. An actor's technique of recreating an emotion on stage by recalling an equivalent experience in his or her life.

See EMOTIONAL RECALL, METHOD ACTING, SENSE MEMORY.

afterpiece. In eighteenth-century London theatres, a short comedy performed after a five-act tragedy, providing comic relief for the audience.

See ANTI-MASQUE.

agitprop. A form of political theatre created by German director Erwin Piscator in the 1920s. Multistage, multimedia productions, using film, slides, placards, and music-hall styles, presented propagandistic drama that was immediately relevant to the audience.

See ALIENATION EFFECT, AVANT-GARDE, DIDACTIC, EPIC THEATRE, GUERRILLA THEATRE, PROPAGANDA PLAY.

agon. A debate. In the Prologue of Greek Old Comedy, a "happy idea" was put forth, then the merits of the idea were argued in the agon. In Aristophanes' *Lysistrata,* for example, the women decide to end war by going on a sex strike. In the agon, Lysistrata and the Magistrate debate the issue. She prevails in the argument and he retreats.

See OLD COMEDY.

Aldwych farce. One of a series of farces by Ben Travers and others that were produced at London's Aldwych Theatre in the 1920s and 1930s. The plays, mainly bedroom farces, featured sexual escapades, especially attempted marital infidelities.

See FARCE, WHITEHALL FARCE.

alexandrine. A line of verse having twelve syllables, with every second syllable stressed (iambic hexameter), favored by writers of neoclassical French tragedy. Twentieth-century American poet Robert Lowell, who translated Racine's *Phaedra,* said the line is impossible to render into English, but even in translation the alexandrine can be seen occasionally:

PHAEDRA: My gloomy frenzy from the world my hell.

See NEOCLASSICISM.

alienation effect. An effect on viewers produced by keeping audience members emotionally uninvolved so that they can recognize and accept the political or philosophical message of the play. Bertolt Brecht devised the technique for his "epic dramas," such as *Mother Courage* and *The Good Woman of Setzuan.* He shattered the illusion of audience members that they were watching real life by interrupting the course of action and lowering the tension. His productions would not allow audience members to maintain aesthetic distance and, instead, forced their attention on his message. The actors in such productions may contribute to the effect by performing with an attitude that comments on the characters instead of realistically reproducing them.

See AGITPROP, AVANT-GARDE, EPIC THEATRE, GUERRILLA THEATRE.

allegory. A work in which there is a one-to-one correspondence between the literal, or surface, meaning and the allegorical, or underlying, meaning. In the medieval play *Everyman,* the protagonist Everyman (standing for all people) undertakes a journey (through life) and asks for companions, but is rejected by all except the one called Good Deeds. In modern times, such works as Thornton Wilder's *The Skin of Our Teeth,* with its cavalcade of human history, Edward Albee's *Seascape,* with its human-sized talking lizards, and Vaclav Havel's *Temptation,* with its retelling of the Faust legend, have been viewed as allegorical.

See ARCHETYPAL CHARACTER, PLOT.

alliteration. The repetition of initial sounds in two or more words in a line. It is a poetic technique sometimes used in verse drama, as in this line from T. S. Eliot's *The Family Reunion:*

CHORUS: And the *s*eason of the *s*tifled *s*orrow.

American College Theatre Festival. An annual competition of college and university productions that begins in local areas and advances to state, regional, and national festivals. Sponsored by the American Theatre Association, the festival names the best production of the year and gives awards for acting, writing, and designing.

See ACADEMIC THEATRE, EDUCATIONAL THEATRE.

American Theatre Wing. The organization that conducts the Tony Awards. It began as a group running canteens for service personnel during World War II. It is now active in educational projects, gives awards, and performs in hospitals.

See ANTOINETTE PERRY AWARDS.

amphitheatre. Originally the Colosseum in Rome, now any large, oval-shaped building with no roof and tiers of spectator seats. The Colosseum was used for gladiator contests, not plays, but subsequent buildings of such shape have been designed and used as theatres with arena staging.

See CENTRAL STAGING, THEATRE-IN-THE-ROUND.

anachronism. A person or thing that is out of place chronologically. A famous anachronism is Shakespeare's stage direction of a clock striking in *Julius Caesar*—there were no striking clocks in ancient Rome. Other examples include an actor in a 1930s play wearing a digital watch, or someone in a Victorian play ad-libbing modern slang.

See DECORUM, PROPS, SET.

anagnorisis. The discovery or recognition scene, an important element in classical drama, but also a staple of much modern drama. In the exodos of Euripides' *Hippolytus,* Theseus learns from Artemis that his dying son Hippolytus had been falsely accused of having violated Phaedra, and then father and son are allowed a last embrace. In Shakespeare's *The Winter's Tale,* King Leontes has his queen, Hermione, long thought dead, returned to him when he learns of her innocence and repents of his earlier misjudgment of her. And, of course, in any number of modern mysteries, the identity of the killer is revealed near the play's end.

See CLIMAX, RECOGNITION SCENE, TURNING POINT.

angel. The financial backer of a production. Formerly, a single wealthy person or a small group of people. Now producers look to large corporations for backing.

angiportum. The alleyway running between two houses representing a street scene in Roman comedy. Characters concealed themselves there to eavesdrop and comment on other characters. The setup was faithfully reproduced in the Bert Shevelove and Larry Gelbart modern musical comedy *A Funny Thing Happened on the Way to the Forum,* based on Plautus' *Haunted House.*

angry young men. A name given to participants in a literary movement in Britain during the 1950s. The name was taken from John Osborne's play *Look Back in Anger.* Playwrights involved railed against the establishment, especially its network of "old boys" linked to each other by their Oxford and Cambridge backgrounds and "posh" accents. Leading exponents in the theatre were Osborne, Arnold Wesker, John Arden, John Whiting, Brendan Behan, and, at least in *A Taste of Honey,* Shelagh Delaney.

See ANTIHERO, AVANT-GARDE.

Annie Oakley. A complimentary ticket to a performance. Named so because of the custom of punching a hole in the ticket to imitate the effect achieved by the famed sharpshooter who shot a hole through tickets in an exhibition.

See COMP, PAPERING THE HOUSE.

antagonist. The character who provides the obstacle to the protagonist's objective in a play. Strictly speaking, the antagonist sets the conflict in motion, but commonly the antagonist is now considered an opponent to the protagonist, and is often the villain in the piece. Examples include Creon's opposition to Antigone in Sophocles' tragedy, and King Claudius's opposition to Hamlet in Shakespeare's play. In Osborne's *Look Back in Anger,* the antagonist is "Them," all the forces that conspire to keep Jimmy Porter in his place.

See ECONOMY OF ROLES, OBJECTIVE, OBSTACLE, PROTAGONIST.

anticlimax. The action following the climactic moment in the play, resulting in a reduction of tension. In Sophocles' *Oedipus at Colonus,* after Theseus accompanies Oedipus to the grove where Oedipus meets his death, Theseus returns to comfort Antigone and Ismene and to provide for their return to Thebes. In Anton Chekhov's *The Cherry Orchard,* after the estate has been sold and the family members scatter to begin their new lives, onto the stage totters the feeble old butler Firs to wail aloud at being left behind. Sometimes the playwright devises an anticlimax for humorous effect. In Eugène Ionesco's *The Bald Soprano,* after the climax of the party-conversation-gone-mad, the Martins are shown sitting quietly and echoing the inane conversation of the Smiths that opened the play.

See CLIMAX, RESOLUTION.

antihero. A protagonist who possesses none of the qualities, such as bravery, honesty, and unselfishness, of the traditional hero. Examples include Manfred in Lord Byron's *Manfred,* Valmont in Christopher Hampton's *Les Liaisons Dangereuses,* and Willy Loman in Arthur Miller's *Death of a Salesman.*

anti-masque. A grotesquely comic prelude to a masque entertainment. This introduction, which involved song, dance, and manic capering about, was drawn in part from mummers' plays and fertility festivals. Ben Jonson created the device, although it owes something to the satyr plays of the Greeks and was probably largely improvisational.

See AFTERPIECE, MASQUE.

antistrophe. The second part of the choral ode, after the strophe and before the epode. In Greek drama, the chorus performed a countermovement in its dance, and there was also a turn of thought at the point of the antistrophe. In Aeschylus' *Eumenides,* the chorus, speaking for the Furies, uses the strophe to describe their pleasure at hunting down and punishing murderers of kin. Then in the antistrophe they insist that they do this only to spare other gods the work.

See CHORUS, EPODE, STROPHE.

Antoinette Perry Awards. Popularly called the Tonys, these mounted silver medallions depicting the masks of comedy and tragedy are awarded each year for the best work in such areas as acting, writing, and design in the New York theatre. The award is named to honor Antoinette Perry, an actor, director, and theatre activist of the 1930s and 1940s. The first Tonys were given in 1947.

See AMERICAN THEATRE WING, TONY AWARDS.

Apollonian. A term used by nineteenth-century German philosopher and critic Friedrich Nietzsche to describe the rationality and control in a work of art. The term is akin to classicism and opposed to dionysian principles, or romanticism. Nietzsche further saw Greek tragedy as the product of the tension between the apollonian and dionysian.

See DIONYSIAN.

apron. The area of the stage in front of the curtain line; also called the *forestage.* In some theatres this may be a platform that can be placed over the pit when a larger acting area is needed.

See ACTING AREA, FORESTAGE, GROUNDLING, PIT, THRUST STAGE.

archetypal character. A character who represents a large group of people sharing the same dream, seeking the same kind of adventures, fighting similar battles, or striving for a particular goal. An archetypal character grows and changes, unlike a stock character, who is static and two-dimensional and who merely fills out the cast and elicits a predictable response. (The stuffy English butler and the dizzy blonde secretary are two stock characters.) John and Mary, the protagonists in Elmer Rice's *Two on an Island,* are examples of archetypal characters—even their names suggest universal qualities. They have come to New York City to pursue success in the theatre. As they embark on Broadway careers, they take risks, suffer setbacks, and face difficult decisions. At the end of the play, they are not the same people as they were at the beginning. Although their adventures are specific and their reactions individual, John and Mary represent all hopefuls in the theatre.

The Tony Award-winning musical *City of Angels* by Larry Gelbart has been called the archetypal private-eye play because its protagonist Stone and his adventures could serve as models for the *genre.*

See ALLEGORY, CHARACTER, MYTH, STOCK CHARACTERS, STOCK RESPONSE.

arc light. A spotlight that uses an electrical current arcing between two carbon rods; loosely, any extremely bright stage light. Low-intensity arc lights are noisy and use direct current only, while the high-intensity arc of today can use alternating current.

See SPOTLIGHT.

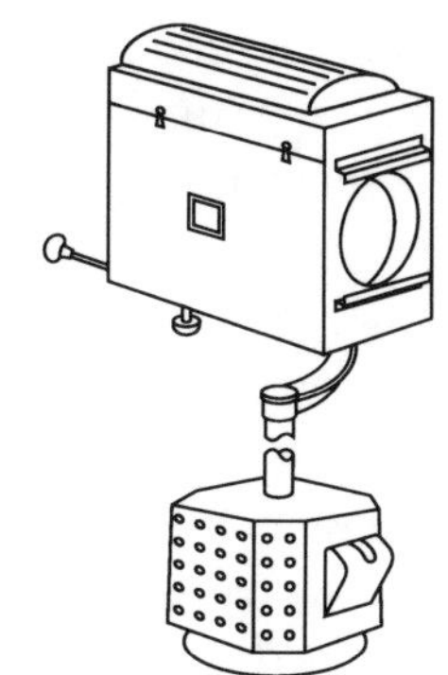

Direct current carbon arc light

arena stage. An open space at floor level with the audience in bleacher-like seats on all sides of the acting area. Also called *theatre-in-the-round* and *central staging,* examples are the Arena Stage in Washington, D.C., and the Circle-in-the-Square in New York City.

See CENTRAL STAGING.

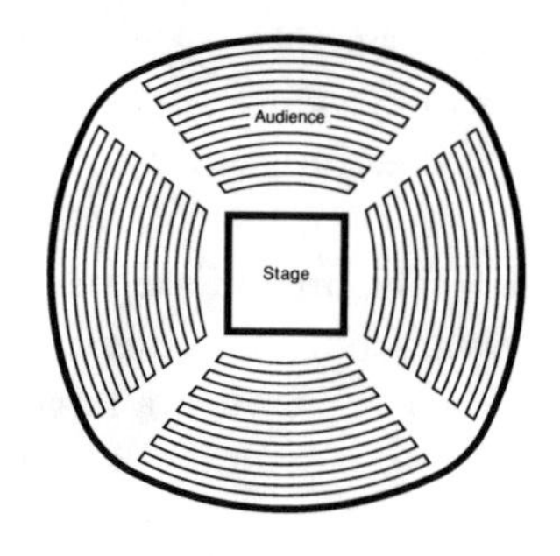

Arena stage

argument. A short statement or summary of what a drama, a book, or a poem is about.

Aristotle's six elements of drama. Also called the Six Elements of Tragedy. In his *Poetics,* Aristotle defines and discusses the six elements that make up the tragedy. Many critics have extended his definition to describe all types of plays.

See CHARACTER, DICTION, MUSIC, PLOT, SPECTACLE, THOUGHT.

Arlecchino, also spelled Harlequino. A character from commedia dell'arte (Italian comedy popular from the sixteenth to the eighteenth centuries) whose persona was that of the wily servant, comical and witty. He eventually metamorphosed into the Harlequin of particolored costume who loved Columbine in English pantomime. One of the best places to see Arlecchino is in Carlo Goldoni's *A Servant of Two Masters,* where among the *lazzi* (tricks) is the juggling of a huge tower of gelatin as Arlecchino attempts to wait on two masters, each in a different dining room.

See COMMEDIA DELL'ARTE, HARLEQUIN, HARLEQUINADE, LAZZO, STOCK CHARACTERS.

arras setting. A set that uses a cyclorama rather than scenery.

See CURTAIN SET, CYCLORAMA.

artistic failure. A production that receives good reviews yet has little commercial success, or one that has some artistic merit yet does not receive good reviews and does not achieve financial success. Stephen Sondheim's *Merrily We Roll Along* reworked material of a George S.

Kaufman and Moss Hart hit play and added a musical score that sold well on records, but the original production and the many attempts at revival have been failures at the box office.

See CRITICISM.

asbestos curtain. A fire-retardant curtain that can be lowered to fill the proscenium arch. It was customary to lower and raise this curtain once during the intermission of each performance. Since the outlawing of asbestos, other fire-retardant substances have been substituted, but the name generally remains the same.

See ACT, CURTAIN.

aside. Words spoken by an actor so that the audience can hear them but, by convention, the other actors cannot. The cliché "Curses, foiled again!" spoken by the villain in melodrama is an example, as is "Remuneration! O, that's the Latin word for three farthings," uttered by Costard when he is handed a coin by Holofernes in Shakespeare's *Love's Labor's Lost.*

See PRESENTATIONAL, SOLILOQUY.

asphaleian system. A stage that is divided into sections, each of which can be raised or lowered individually by a hydraulic lift. Such a stage is used in the Denver Center of Performing Arts, Colorado.

See EXPRESSIONISM, STAGE.

audition. n., The opportunity to read for a part in a play; v., the act of reading for a part in a play. In the case of a musical, an audition will include singing and dancing for the director and his or her associates. The audition may also require the actor to present a prepared monolog.

See CALL BACK, COLD READING, MONOLOG, ROLE.

auditorium. The part of the theatre building that holds the audience, also called the *house.* The term may also refer to the entire theatre plant, as in a school auditorium.

See HOUSE, THEATRON.

auto-sacramentales. Spanish religious plays of the sixteenth to eighteenth centuries. Though later than the English mystery plays, auto-sacramentales are equivalent in subject and form. Also, like the English cycle plays, they were often presented on the Feast of Corpus

Christi. Pedro Calderon was the outstanding playwright of the genre and was responsible for all those staged in Madrid.

See CORPUS CHRISTI PLAYS, CYCLE PLAYS, MYSTERY PLAY.

avant-garde. Literally, the advance guard, especially in the arts. In each theatrical movement, the avant-garde are those on the cutting edge whose work is usually experimental and unorthodox. In this century, such groups as La Mama Troupe in New York City, Jerzy Grotowski's Polish Lab Theatre in Poland, and Antonin Artaud's Theatre of Cruelty in France are considered the avant-garde. Other examples include Megan Terry *(Viet Rock)* and Heiner Mueller (whose eight-hour *The Hamlet Machine* features mixed-media presentations and themes of anger and dissatisfaction with the status quo).

See ABSURD THEATRE OF, ALIENATION, CRUELTY THEATRE OF, DADAISM, EXISTENTIALISM, GUERRILLA THEATRE, HAPPENING, KITCHEN SINK DRAMA, OFF BROADWAY, POOR THEATRE.

avista. The process of changing the scenery in full view of the audience. This may be done by a stage crew uniformly dressed all in black and working in 20 percent light, or by crew members in ordinary working clothes in full light.

See STAGE CREW.

B

back cloth. British term for backdrop.

backdrop. A flat surface the width of the stage, usually made of canvas, hanging from the flies at the rear of the staging area and painted to represent the desired setting. When painted to represent the sky, it's called the *sky drop.*

backing. Flats, screens, and drops used backstage to mask the audience's sight lines through the doors and windows of the set. Also, the financial support needed to produce a play.

See ANGEL, FLAT, MASK, SIGHT LINES.

backstage. The area behind the set or backdrop that is not seen by the audience. May also include the wings.

bagline. The heavy, four-stranded hemp rope attached to a sandbag and used to lift the bag while tying it to other bags in the same group in order to lift a unit of scenery.

See SCENERY.

ballad opera. A production in which sections of dialog alternate with lyrics set to already-popular songs. An eighteenth-century example is

John Gay's *The Beggar's Opera.* More recently the Olivier Award-winning musical *Return to the Forbidden Planet* by Bob Carlton offers a science fiction version of Shakespeare's *The Tempest* with interpolations of popular songs from the 1950s and 1960s.

barker. A spokesman, often in costume, who stands at the entrance to a show to attract customers by a loud and flamboyant sales pitch.

barn door. A device consisting of two or four hinged metal flaps placed in front of a spotlight and manipulated to change the light beam pattern into any number of shapes.
See SPOTLIGHT.

barnstorming. Touring small towns to perform, using anything from barns to town squares as playing areas.
See BUS AND TRUCK COMPANY.

barrel system. A method of moving scenery, also known as drum and shaft because a rope is attached to a cylindrical shaft that is turned by a lever.
See DRUM AND SHAFT, SCENERY.

batten. A horizontal pipe suspended from the flies, on which scenery and lights may be hung. A batten system consists of counterweighted battens on a pulley system that can be raised or lowered over the entire staging area.
See FLIES, SCENERY.

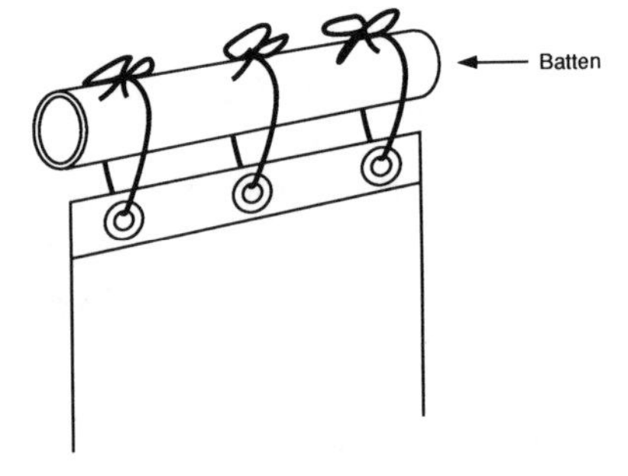

beat. The length of a pause between words, speeches, or actions. One beat is roughly equivalent to a count of one. Also used to describe the tempo of a scene.
See TEMPO.

beginners. The actors who appear on stage when the play begins or shortly thereafter. The stage manager usually calls, "Beginners, please," at five minutes to curtain.

below. To be downstage of someone or something.
See DOWNSTAGE.

biomechanics. A theory of early-twentieth-century Russian director Vsevolod Meyerhold that actors can use certain patterns of muscular activity to elicit a particular emotion; for example, to express joy the actor could turn a somersault. This was in opposition to the Stanislavski method, which asked actors to find the motivation for an emotion from something inside themselves.
See AFFECTIVE MEMORY.

bit, bit part. A small role consisting of a very few lines and a brief appearance on stage.
See LINES, ROLE.

black box. A small theatre of oblong shape but without a proscenium arch. The interior is painted black: walls, floor, ceiling, and horizontal or vertical drapes are all black.

blackout. A lighting cue that requires the lighting technician to totally darken the entire stage in a split second. This is usually done at the end of a scene to provide a startling effect.
See LIGHTING PLOT.

blackout sketch. A short performance, usually comic, requiring instantaneous darkening of the entire stage to punctuate the punchline. Commonly used in burlesque.
See BURLESQUE.

blank verse. Lines of unrhymed iambic pentameter (poetic feet consisting of one unstressed syllable followed by one stressed syllable and arranged five to a line) used by writers of verse drama. Critics refer to "Marlowe's mighty line" because of his skillful use of it in such plays as *Doctor Faustus:*

> FAUSTUS: Was this the face that launched a thousand ships
> And burnt the topless towers of Ilium?

bleeding. A scene-painting technique that uses a bright coat of paint that will partially show through a lighter top coat on a flat. Also, in a lay-

out drawing, key points are inked in with dye so they will bleed through the base coat and serve as a guide to later detail painting.
See FLAT.

blocking. Determining the basic movements of the actors during a play. Some of this is provided by the playwright in stage directions, and some is developed by the actors through a careful reading of the lines, but the majority is supplied by the director and includes entrances, exits, and crosses.
See DIRECTOR, STAGE DIRECTIONS.

bloom. Reflection from a mirror or other highly polished surface on stage.

boards. The stage. To "tread the boards" is to appear on stage.
See ACTING AREA, DECK, STAGE.

boat truck. A wagon or low platform, running on casters, on which whole units of scenery can be moved on and off stage.
See SCENERY, WAGON.

bombast. Speech that is too emotional or inflated for the occasion. Literally, cotton stuffing. There are many examples in the speeches of Falstaff in Shakespeare's *Henry IV, Part I* and in the pretentiousness of Don Armado in *Love's Labor's Lost.* Most recently in the Alain Boublil and Claude-Michel Schoenberg musical *Miss Saigon,* the young soldier Chris runs around frantically crying out for his "bride" when there has been nothing to indicate he thinks of her as anything but a temporary lover.
See DIALOG.

book. The script of the play. A "book show" is a musical with a plot as opposed to a revue, a series of unrelated or only thematically linked sketches.
See LIBRETTO, REVUE.

booked flat. Two flats lashed together and opened at an angle to form a V.
See FLAT.

boom. Also called *boomerang,* a vertical pipe used to mount a spotlight. Also a pole used to extend a microphone out over a set.

See SPOTLIGHT.

border. A short drape hung above the stage to mask the flies when the set does not contain a ceiling.

See GRAND DRAPE.

border lights. A strip of lights hung above the stage and at the front to provide illumination for the whole acting area.

boulevard drama. A type of play originating in nineteenth-century France that exemplified the spirit of the materialistic, irreverent, pleasure-seeking young men-about-town of Paris. The form included both farce and domestic drama and may be seen in such plays of Eugene Labiche (now in the permanent repertoire of the Comédie-Française) as *The Italian Straw Hat,* and the operettas of Jacques Offenbach.

See FARCE.

bounce. To reflect light off the floor or walls of the set.

See EFFECTS.

bourgeois drama. Eighteenth-century pseudo-serious plays about middle-class society with emphasis on pathos and morality. Also called *comédie larmoyante* and *sentimental comedy,* the form is best represented by Denis Diderot's *Le Père de Famille* in France and George Lillo's *George Barnwell* in England.

See DOMESTIC TRAGEDY.

bowdlerize. To expurgate indecent or indelicate portions of a literary work. The term comes from Thomas Bowdler who published Shakespeare's works and cut from them anything he considered unfit to be read by his family.

box set. A setting of three walls and a ceiling, leaving the fourth wall to be imagined by the actors. The doors and windows are practical, and as nearly as possible the set represents a real room.

See PRACTICAL SCENERY, REPRESENTATIONAL.

boy companies. Young boys of the English royal choirs who often acted in plays at the court during the sixteenth century. The boys had something of a professional status and appeared in plays by Ben Jonson and John Lyly.

brace. Stage brace. A rod hooked to the back of a flat at one end and weighted or screwed down to the floor at the other end.

break. To fold or unfold scenery.

break a leg. A traditional greeting to an actor, given just before a performance. Born of the superstition that if one wishes "good luck," the perverse gods will send the opposite, but if one wishes misfortune, the gods will be tricked into sending an actor good luck.

breakaway. Scenery or props rigged to break on cue. Includes such things as windowpanes made of candy glass, dishes prebroken and then lightly glued together, and stair railings prebroken, lightly glued together, and backed with thin strips of orange crate to provide appropriate sound effects when broken on stage.

See EFFECTS, PROPS.

bridge. A mechanical device for lifting large pieces of scenery. Formerly devised of counterweights and a crank with a handle, most bridges are now electronically controlled. The Andrew Lloyd Webber–Tim Rice musical *Starlight Express* uses a bridge to move the roller skating ramps in and out of play.

bridle. A set of lines evenly spaced over the length of a batten to support it.

See BATTEN.

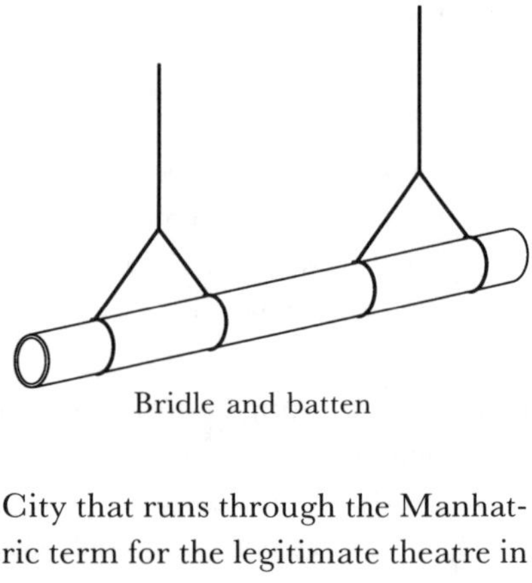

Bridle and batten

brighten. A direction to an actor to read a line with more liveliness.

Broadway. A boulevard in New York City that runs through the Manhattan theatre district. Also, the generic term for the legitimate theatre in

New York City, as in the phrase "making it on Broadway," meaning gaining success as an actor.

See ACTORS' EQUITY, TONY AWARDS.

brush out. A term referring to that middle ground between a blackout and a fade.

See LIGHTING PLOT.

bull line. The heavy rope used on a winch to lift counterweighted scenery.

bumper. A low platform backstage against which the boat truck can bump. Also a metal hoop on a lighting batten to protect it from flying scenery.

See BOAT TRUCK.

bump up. To raise quickly the intensity of stage lighting.

burlesque. A type of comedy in which characters, stage business, dialog, and costumes are so exaggerated as to destroy any illusion of reality. In the seventeenth to the nineteenth centuries, such plays were used to parody some popular fashion or work of art. In the twentieth century, the word *burlesque* was also used to describe a kind of theatrical revue that featured skits, comic routines, songs, dances, and even striptease performers. Stephen Sondheim's *Gypsy* was a musical version of Gypsy Rose Lee's account of her experiences in burlesque.

See COMEDY, EXTRAVAGANZA, FARCE.

bus and truck company. A troupe of actors performing around the country, using a bus for the players and a truck for their costumes and scenery, often playing single-night engagements in small towns.

See BARNSTORMING.

business, stage business. All the actions, excluding blocking, performed by the actors on stage, such as gesturing, opening doors or windows, serving food, writing letters, embracing, unpacking, drawing a weapon. Some of these are suggested by the playwright in the book, some arise organically out of the lines of the play, and some are given to the actor by the director.

See IMPLICIT DIRECTIONS, SMALL WORK, STAGE DIRECTIONS.

buskin. The thick-soled, laced, leather boot worn by actors in Greek tragedy to give them added height and, thereby, dignity; also called cothurnus.

byplay. An action that takes place to the side while the main action of the play goes on. In Tina Howe's *Coastal Disturbances,* Holly and the lifeguard Leo are conducting an uneasy and tentative courtship at the beach while in the background two children shout at each other over a tin-can-and-string phone system. The byplay catches the attention of the audience and adds to the humor of the scene but does not completely distract from the main action.

See PASSION PLAYS.

cabaret. A nightclub that features song and dance and comedy acts while patrons dine and drink. Also, the entertainment offered. The scale of the production may range from an abbreviated version of a musical comedy to a lavish revue.

See REVUE.

call back. The second stage in the audition process in which actors who appeared for the initial reading and who are now under serious consideration for the roles to be cast are asked to return for further readings or interviews or both.

See AUDITION.

call board. A bulletin board placed backstage upon which schedules, announcements, and even reviews are posted for the cast and crew.

canon. The entire body of work by a given playwright.

cape-and-sword play. Spanish comedy featuring swordplay, disguises, gallant lovers, and beautiful ladies of the nobility, all in an elegant setting. Lope de Vega (1562–1635) was a leading practitioner of the form.

carnival mass (play). A type of work originally designed to be performed on Shrove Tuesday, the last day before Lent begins. The play uses elements of Catholic liturgy, social morality, music from the Catholic Mass, masks, puppets, and characters such as the wise-fool. Dating from the fifteenth century and found in many Christian cultures, the type has been newly realized in the Julie Taymor–Elliot Goldenthal creation *Juan Darien.*

See CHURCH DRAMA, ECCLESIASTICAL DRAMA, MASK.

carriage and frame. A system for changing the scenery wings (sidepieces used with a back cloth instead of a box set). The wings are mounted on a unit controlled by a set of carriages, or platforms, on casters, one of which moves a wing offstage while another moves a wing onstage.

cast. All the actors performing in a given play.

See DRAMATIS PERSONAE.

casting. The process of auditions and interviews by which the director selects the actors to play the roles in a play.

See AUDITION.

catastrophe. More commonly called the denouement, or resolution, this section of a play contains the unknotting of the entanglements of the plot. This may involve, for example, revelation of the identity of the stranger, a reversal of fortunes for the protagonist, or a reconciliation of the estranged lovers. The term was used by nineteenth-century German critic Gustav Freytag in his analysis of the typical structure of a five-act play.

See DENOUEMENT, RESOLUTION.

catharsis, katharsis. The feeling of release at the end of a tragedy experienced by audience members who have undergone feelings of fear and pity, shared in the troubles of the play's protagonist, and now are set free from the emotional grasp of the action. Aristotle called this cleansing the pleasure of tragedy.

See TRAGEDY.

catwalk. A narrow metal bridge up in the flies by which the stage crew can reach and adjust the hung scenery.

See FLIES.

ceiling cloth. Canvas stretched out over the top of a box set and functioning as a ceiling for the room represented.
See BOX SET.

cellar. The space immediately under the stage that contains scenery-changing machinery and the trap chamber for the trapdoor.
See TRAP.

centering. An actor's term for concentrating, focusing on the work at hand, and being in character, in the moment of the play.

center stage. Literally, the space at the very center of the acting area. Also, slang for being the focus of the audience's attention.

central action. The series of events presented in a play. What Aristotle called simply the action or the general movement of the plot.

central staging. A method of presenting a play on an area that is surrounded on all sides by the audience. Also called arena stage. Actors gain access to the stage down aisles through the audience.
See ARENA STAGE.

chamber play. A play written to be performed or merely read aloud, in a room rather than onstage, and for an audience of friends rather than for paying customers.

character. A person in a play, or the personality of that person. Aristotle called character, along with thought, that aspect of plot from which the action arises.
See ROLE.

character role. A major role in a play, but not one of the romantic leads. Often used to mean a character unlike the actor playing the role in terms of age, voice, or physical characteristics. Also used for elderly and funny characters, for example, Sir Toby Belch in Shakespeare's *Twelfth Night,* Lady Bracknell in Oscar Wilde's *The Importance of Being Earnest,* and the elder Churches in Tina Howe's *Painting Churches.*
See CONFIDANT, FOIL.

cheat. To turn the body out, partially toward the audience, while appearing to talk directly to another character onstage. There is no disapproval expressed by the term. When actors are too honest—and face each other directly—their facial expressions cannot be seen by the audience, and their voice projection may be muffled.

chew the scenery. To overact, indulge in histrionics, flail about, gesture too broadly, or behave in an emotional manner, all out of proportion to the content of the scene.

See HAM, HISTRIONICS.

chiaroscuro. The interplay of light and shadow as used in stage lighting and in scene painting. It may be used to create atmosphere and mood, or used symbolically to depict emotional content. In the case of minimal setting, chiaroscuro may be used to create the effect of buildings, jail bars, or trees.

See EFFECTS, MINIMAL SETTING.

choices. The decisions of the actor or director as to the way a character in a play will be interpreted in a given production, or even in a given performance within a run. An actor playing the governess Madrigal in Enid Bagnold's *The Chalk Garden* may opt for a tight-lipped, guarded portrayal, or for a bland, deceptively open and smiling impersonation. Most directors prefer to let actors explore their choices before deciding on what will best serve the show.

choregus. Title given to a wealthy citizen in ancient Greece who was selected to pay for the training and costumes of the chorus in dramas.

See CHORUS, CLASSICAL DRAMA.

choreographer. The person who designs the dance steps to be used in a play. Some, such as Agnes De Mille, Bob Fosse, and Tommy Tune, have established immediately recognizable styles of dancing in their choreography and have strongly influenced the development of dance in musical plays.

chorus. In Greek drama, the group of performers who sang and danced between the episodes of the play. The chorus also narrated the offstage action, commented on events, even moralized on them, as in Sophocles' *Antigone* when the chorus first rejoices in the defeat of the Argive army, then comments that Polynices was a traitor deserving of his fate. The term *chorus* is now commonly used to designate a group of performers who sing, dance, or recite together in a production.

See CLASSICAL DRAMA.

chorus character. A single character who functions as a chorus in a play, that is, narrates or comments on the action. The Stage Manager in Thornton Wilder's *Our Town* is such a character, as are some of Shakespeare's fools.

See PRESENTATIONAL.

chronicle play. A play with a historical basis, told as a series of episodes rather than as a complete story with a structured plot. Shakespeare's *Richard II,* based on Raphael Holinshed's *Chronicles,* is an example.

See HISTORY PLAY.

church drama. Generally, drama based on religious subjects. Specifically, the Christian church in medieval to Reformation times as a force in presenting and formulating plays. In the twentieth century, the revival seen in the plays of T. S. Eliot, Charles Williams, and Dorothy Sayers, and the dramatizations of the works of C. S. Lewis and other Christian apologists.

See CARNIVAL MASS, CORPUS CHRISTI PLAYS, CYCLE PLAYS, MYSTERY PLAY.

circus. Popularly, a traveling show with high wire and animal acts, clowns, and trapeze artists, although the Cirque du Soleil does not use animals. Originally, the arena in which Roman chariot races and gladiator contests took place, for example, the Colosseum in Rome.

claque. Friends and relatives of the actors or people paid by the theatre management to attend a show and respond enthusiastically so that critics and others in the audience will think the actors and the play are popular.

See COMP.

classical drama. Formally, the drama of ancient Greece and Rome. Popularly, any play written before the present century that has stood the test of time. Actors auditioning are often asked to prepare two monologs, one classical and one modern.

See ARISTOTLE'S SIX ELEMENTS OF DRAMA, CHORUS.

clewing. Holding several ropes together by knots or a clew (loop), so that they can be handled as a single line, in rigging.
See SCENERY.

climax. The point of highest intensity in the action of a play, preceded by the rising action and followed by the falling action. In Caryl Churchill's *Top Girls,* such a point is reached in the first scene of act 2 when sixteen-year-old Angie runs away from home to visit her "Auntie" Marlene at the Top Girls employment agency. Angie suspects and the audience knows that Marlene is actually Angie's mother and the whole action of the play has led up to this climactic moment.
See ANTICLIMAX, CRISIS.

closet drama. A play written to be read, but not to be performed. Popular in the Romantic age among such poets as Percy Shelley *(Prometheus Bound),* Johann Goethe *(Faust),* and Lord Byron *(Manfred).*
See CHAMBER PLAY.

cloth. Any large, unframed piece of canvas intended for scenery.
See CEILING CLOTH, DROP.

cloud border. A narrow piece of cloth used at the top of the stage to mask the flies from the audience. May be cut into shapes at the lower edge to resemble clouds, for example, or trees.

clown character. A comic character who may be simpleminded, an ironic commentator, or an actual jester. Shown in Shakespeare's plays by, respectively, Costard in *Love's Labours Lost,* Jaques in *As You Like It,* and Feste in *Twelfth Night.* In the commedia dell'arte, Arlecchino, the wily servant, is a clown character. In the twentieth century, Tom in Ann Jellicoe's *The Knack* combines all three elements as he at times capers about in a silly manner, at other times comments ironically on the action, and finally acts as jester to the triumphant Colin.
See ARLECCHINO, BURLESQUE, COMEDY, COMMEDIA DELL'ARTE, FARCE, STOCK CHARACTERS.

cold reading. An audition where the actor is asked to read from a script without any preparation. Many directors prefer this to a prepared reading, feeling they are able to see more of the actor's potential and range.
See AUDITION.

collaborative theatre. A situation in which the actors and director work together to develop the script for a play. A popular example is *A Chorus Line,* for which dancers met with choreographer Michael Bennett to discuss their experiences auditioning and performing. From tapes of those sessions, Bennett and James Kirkwood fashioned the book for the show. *The Me Nobody Knows* used a collection of writings by inner-city children intertwined with a soft rock musical score by Gary William Friedman. In other instances, a playwright may workshop a play with the actors contributing ideas as the rehearsals go along.

See ACADEMIC THEATRE, WORKSHOP.

Columbine. A character from the commedia dell'arte. At first a pert maidservant, she gradually became the daughter, or ward, or even wife of Pantaloon. She loves Harlequin and eventually elopes with him, but is often presented as unhappy in love. The traditional Columbine mask has teardrops painted below the eyes.

See ARLECCHINO, COMMEDIA DELL'ARTE, INGENUE, STOCK CHARACTERS.

comedy. Generally, a play of a happy nature, lightness of spirit, and amusing dialog, in which serious disaster is averted. The term may also mean, in contrast to tragedy, any play that does not end unhappily. There are comedies of manners, such as the plays of Noel Coward, and romantic comedies, such as Shakespeare's *A Midsummer Night's Dream* and John van Druten's *The Voice of the Turtle.* Although comedy may be designed primarily to entertain, many playwrights may include thought-provoking elements, as does William Saroyan in *The Time of Your Life.* Ancient Greek comedy began with the fantastical devices in Aristophanes' *Frogs, Clouds,* and *Birds,* and evolved to the lovers' adventures of Menander and the Romans Plautus and Terence. Plautus' *The Twin Menaechmi* became the model for Shakespeare's *The Comedy of Errors,* and later the Richard Rodgers–Lorenz Hart musical *The Boys From Syracuse.*

See BURLESQUE, FARCE.

comedy of humors. Best seen in Ben Jonson's work, this type of play satirizes the dominant trait of the principal character, such as the greed of Jonson's Volpone.

See STOCK CHARACTERS.

comedy of manners. Satirizes the manners and mores of a given segment of society. May be seen in the witty plays of Restoration playwrights William Congreve and Richard Sheridan. In this century, such plays include Phillip Barry's *Holiday* and *Philadelphia Story,* and Noel Coward's *Private Lives* and *Design for Living.* Currently, comedy of manners is written by A. G. Gurney and Alan Ayckbourn.

See DRAWING ROOM COMEDY.

comes down. Slang expression for the time a show finishes each evening. The term derives from the curtain coming down at the end. Also used for the closing of a show.

comic opera. Usually an opera with a comic plot, Johann Strauss, Jr.'s *Die Fledermaus,* for example. May also refer to a drama, essentially serious or romantic in nature, but with songs and comic episodes, such as the operettas of early-twentieth-century composers Victor Herbert, Sigmund Romberg, and Rudolph Friml.

See OPERETTA.

comic relief. A break in the tension of a tragedy provided by a comic character—for example, the drunken porter in *Macbeth* grumbling as he opens the door to Macduff and Lennox. Also, a comic episode—the grave diggers in *Hamlet* with their disputation on Christian burial. The break serves to relax the audience momentarily in preparation for the dramatic upsurge to follow. It may even be as brief as Mercutio's wry comment on the extent of his wound in *Romeo and Juliet:*

> " 'Tis not so deep as a well, nor so wide as a church door,
> but 'tis enough, 'twill serve."

See TENSION.

command performance. A performance by an acting company before a royal person, at his or her request. Now such occasions are often used as fund-raisers for charity.

commedia dell'arte. Sixteenth-to-eighteenth-century Italian comedy, originally improvisational, but eventually using set bits of business called *lazzi.* Each troupe of players developed and jealously guarded its own lazzi and passed them down from parents to children. The basic plots were derived from Roman comedy and the cast of stock characters included Arlecchino, Columbine, Pierrot, Pantaloon, Punchinello, Pagliaccio, and Scaramouche. The players appeared masked and in costumes that became conventions of the genre. Today we see the remnants of commedia types in such stock characters as the know-it-all English butler (Arlecchino), the pert French maid (Columbine), the macho athlete (Scaramouche), and the hen-pecked husband (Punchinello).

See ARLECCHINO, COLUMBINE, IMPROVISATION, LAZZO, PANTALOON, PIERROT, PUNCHINELLO, SCARAMOUCHE, STOCK CHARACTERS.

community theatre. Amateur productions by residents of a locality, cast at open auditions or from an established group of volunteers. Such theatre is usually nonprofit and relies on a repertoire of popular favorites rather than experimental new pieces. Increasingly, such theatres are hiring professional directors and house managers.

comp. A complimentary ticket to a show. "To comp" someone is to provide a free ticket for that person to attend a specific performance.

See ANNIE OAKLEY, PAPERING THE HOUSE.

company. A group of actors and technicians who join together to present plays. The organization may be democratic, with voting to determine the plays to be done, or it may have a director in charge of such decisions. Either way, the members function as a team.

company switch. A portable distribution panel with hookup terminals, used to supply power for lighting in a traveling show. The panel receives power from a generator or pole and feeds it to the lighting equipment. May also be permanently located at the side of the proscenium for the connection of portable control boards.

See BUS AND TRUCK COMPANY.

complication. Any incident that further tangles the plot. In classical drama, any opposition to the protagonist. The second act of a five-act tragedy is often called the "act of complication." In Carson McCullers' *The Member of the Wedding,* Frankie's longing to go with her brother and his fiancée when they return to Winter Hill begins to complicate the plot.

See PLOT.

conceit. A finely wrought phrase, often an extended metaphor. In excess, an overly elaborate analogy. Shakespeare has Romeo say of Juliet: "She hangs upon the cheek of night like a rich jewel in an Ethiop's ear—beauty too rich for use, for earth too dear." More briefly, in the *Importance of Being Earnest,* Oscar Wilde has Lady Bracknell inform John Worthing, "An engagement should come on a young girl as a surprise, pleasant or unpleasant as the case may be."

concentration. The actor's focus on the moment of the play in which he or she is acting. Stanislavski urged his actors to concentrate on a specific objective in each scene.

See CENTERING.

confidant (fem., confidante). A close friend of the principal character to whom he or she confides private thoughts, fears, longing. The device enables the playwright to reveal such thoughts without having the principal character speak a soliloquy. The confidant becomes the "side-kick" in modern plays, and the confidante often becomes the soubrette. Examples are Celia to Rosalind in Shakespeare's *As You Like It* and Virgil to Bo in William Inge's *Bus Stop.*

See FOIL, SOUBRETTE.

conflict. The opposition to the protagonist in a play. The opposition may be of equal strength as in man against man, woman against woman, team against team, country against country; it may be of unequal strength as in a man or woman against society, the world, the gods; it may be the psychological conflict of a man or woman vs. the inner self.

See OBJECTIVE, OBSTACLE.

connection. The interdependence of actor to actor in a performance. In a strong connection, there is attention, response, and intuition about what the other actor is thinking and feeling.

constructivism. A concept in stage design, expoused by twentieth-century Russian director Vsevolod Meyerhold, in which the illusion of scenery is created by the juxtapositioning of ladders, scaffolding, and platforms to suggest houses, factories, and public buildings.

See MINIMAL SETTING.

contamination. The use of parts of two different plays to create a third. Often done in Roman times, particularly by Plautus and Terence, using two classical Greek plays. The term has been extended to include Renaissance playwrights who rewrote older plays or borrowed largely from them. Shakespeare's *Troilus and Cressida* owes much to earlier accounts by Chaucer and Boccaccio. Terence's *The Brothers* was based on Menander's *The Brothers* and *The Suicide Pact.*

convention. An implied agreement by the audience to accept an artistic reality for an everyday reality. Like other art forms, drama depends for its effectiveness on certain conventions. The stage itself is a convention, generally a three-sided set that represents both indoor and outdoor scenes. The audience accepts this partial representation of reality, using its imagination to complete the illusion. Another use of an agreement with the audience may be seen in the ways a horse is represented on stage: In Kabuki it is a wooden frame with four legs; in English pantomime two men share a horse costume; morris dancers ride a "hobby horse," or broomstick with a cloth horse's head; in Peter Shaffer's *Equus,* actors wearing hooves and wire-frame headpieces act the horses. In each case the audience understands what is suggested and accepts it.

See MASK, MULTIPLE SETTINGS.

copyright. The playwright's legal ownership and control over production of his or her play in public, and over reproduction in print of whole or huge portions of the script. After seventy-five years, most works are in the public domain and can be printed or performed by anyone without the permission of the author.

Corpus Christi plays. Cycle plays presented outdoors on the Catholic feast day of Corpus Christi, in England during the Middle Ages. These plays were often written in English rather than Latin, and were performed on platforms or wagons in the town square. Best known of the cycle plays is *The Second Shepherd's Play* about a group of shepherds in the hills near Bethlehem on the night Christ was born.

See CARNIVAL MASS, CHURCH DRAMA, CYCLE PLAYS, MYSTERY PLAY.

costume. Clothing worn by the actors in a performance. In period pieces, sometimes called costume dramas, this may mean everything from the skin out. Costumes can represent time and place as well as the income, temperament, and even the state of mind of a character, and can range from actual garments from the period of the play, or recreations of them, to mere suggestions of the period by cut and ornamentation.

See WARDROBE MISTRESS.

costume shop. The room(s) where the costumes for a play are "built." Also, the storage space for the costumes, try-on areas for the actors, and the location of the machinery (washers, dryers, mangles, ironing boards, irons, and sewing machines) needed to keep costumes in good repair.

See WARDROBE MISTRESS.

cothurnus. High-soled boot.

See BUSKIN.

counterweight system. Mechanical system of pulleys, ropes, and weights, such as sandbags, used to hang scenery. The scenery is at one end of a rope, the counterweight at the other. A stagehand, operating from the stage floor, can lift the scenery by pulling on the weighted end of the rope.

See FLIES, SCENERY.

couplet. Two consecutive lines of verse that rhyme. Sometimes used in verse drama. The couplet is very much in evidence in John Heywood's sixteenth-century *The Play Called the Four PP:*

> PARDONER: By the first part of this last tale
> It seemeth you came late from the ale.

Other examples may be found in twentieth-century American poet Richard Wilbur's translation of Moliere's *Tartuffe:*

> DORINE: Surely it is a shame and a disgrace
> To see this man usurp the master's place.

W. B. Yeats, in *The Only Jealousy of Emer,* used couplets for the Ghost of Cuchulain:

> A woman danced and a hawk flew,
> I held out arms and hands, but you
> That now seem friendly flew away
> Half woman and half bird of prey.

crash box. A narrow, high-sided wooden box, with a lead weight at the bottom, placed just offstage, into which an actor or the prop person can hurl a glass or plate to create the sound of breakage.
See EFFECTS, PROPERTIES MANAGER.

create a role. To be the first actor to play a role in its premier performance. Often, such an actor sets the standard or style for all actors who follow in that role. Examples are Carol Channing in *Gentlemen Prefer Blondes,* Alan Bates in *Butley,* and Noel Coward and Gertrude Lawrence in *Private Lives.*

crescendo. The increasing tempo of a play building to the climax. In Aeschylus' *Agamemnon,* Agamemnon's voice is heard from outside the palace calling for help. The chorus dithers about what is happening and what to do. The tension builds until at last the inner doors are opened and Agamemnon is shown lying dead.
See CLIMAX.

crisis. Often used interchangeably with *climax,* this term actually denotes the moment when the choice is made that makes the climax inevitable. The "drama of crisis" shows the fateful act at the beginning of the play, or has it occur before the action of the play, and then withholds the knowledge of it from the protagonist until the climax. Such is the case in Sophocles' *Oedipus Rex.* The rulers of Thebes were warned by the Delphic Oracle that a son would be born who would slay his father and marry his mother. This knowledge and the identity of his true parents is kept from Oedipus until the climax of the play.
See CLIMAX, DRAMATIC IRONY.

criticism. An evaluation and analysis of a play according to accepted aesthetic principles. Criticism differs from reviewing, in which a work is either praised or deprecated according to the personal taste of the reviewer. Respected drama critics through the years include Aristotle, John Dryden, and William Archer. Among Americans are John Gassner and Brooks Atkinson, and recently Edith Oliver and Mimi Kramer of *The New Yorker.*
See ARTISTIC FAILURE.

cross. A stage direction meaning to move across the stage from one side to the other. To "cross down" means to cross over while moving downstage.

See STAGE DIRECTIONS.

cross fade. To fade or dim the lighting from one setup of the lighting control board—that is, one group of pre-set levers to light a given scene to another setup of the board, without completely dimming all the stage lights. One set of lighting cues simply blends into the next.

See LIGHTING PLOT.

cruelty, theatre of. A theory of playwright Antonin Artaud, which he put into practice with his own theatre company in the 1930s. He believed that actors and audiences should be "victims burned at the stake, signaling through the flames." In general this means the presentation of plays that strive to shock the audience into an awareness of the ruthlessness and savagery of existence by showing characters of extremely unconventional behavior. The best-known work in this genre is Peter Weiss's *The Persecution and Assassination of Jean-Paul Marat As Performed by the Inmates of the Asylum of Charenton Under the Direction of the Marquis de Sade,* often simply called *Marat/Sade.*

See AVANT-GARDE.

cue. A signal from the stage manager to actor, stage crew, props manager, or lighting technician that some predetermined action, such as an entrance, sound effects, scenery change, or lighting change, is required. Also used by actors to mean the line immediately before their own. In this sense, "to cue" someone means to supply that line so the actor can say his or her own in a rehearsal.

curtain. Literally, the drape in a proscenium arch theatre that closes off the stage from the audience's view. Also called the house curtain. It may be raised and lowered or opened side-to-side at the end of scenes, acts, or the play itself. In nonproscenium theatres, the blackout of all stage lighting is used in place of the curtain to signal such endings.

curtain line. The last line of the scene; serves as a signal to bring down the curtain. It is often something startling that arouses suspense for the next scene. In comedies it is often a laugh line. At the end of the play, the curtain line is usually a comment on what has happened, a hint that all may not be as it seems, or something shocking as in August Strindberg's *Miss Julie,* which ends with Jean, the valet commanding Julie to "Go!" as he sends her to her suicide.

curtain raiser. A one-act play presented before the main play of the performance. It may be something similar in tone to set the mood, or it may be something quite dissimilar to form a contrast. Peter Shaffer's short play *White Lies* always preceded his *Black Comedy* in its Broadway run.

curtain set. A simple way of dressing the stage in place of elaborate scenery. Side and back drapes are used. Often used for reader's theatre. May be used with one or two small pieces of furniture—a chair to suggest a sitting room, a potted plant to suggest a garden—and is then usually called minimal setting. Thornton Wilder's *Our Town* uses such a setting to good effect: a plank on sawhorses to suggest a soda fountain, for example.

cycle plays. Short plays drawn from Bible stories and presented in medieval England. Also called mystery plays. Several performed at the same program formed a cycle. There are four cycles for which manuscripts exist: York, Chester, Coventry, and Wakefield. The last is the most famous and its thirty-two surviving plays are readily available in print. It was the custom for the town's trade guilds each to sponsor one of the stories, for example, the boatwrights sponsored the story of Noah's Ark; the bakers, the Last Supper; the goldsmiths, the presentation of gifts by the Magi.

See CARNIVAL MASS, CORPUS CHRISTI PLAYS, CHURCH DRAMA.

cyclorama (cyc for short). A fabric drape hung from a semicircular track in the flies that creates a curved backdrop for performances. It may be in a neutral color that can be changed by lighting, or it may be a sky blue for outside settings. Rear projection equipment placed backstage can be used to project images—leaves, clouds, or a city skyline—onto the cyc to create additional settings. The term may also refer to a curved wall at the back of the stage. The cyc curtain may also be used behind a set to provide a finish to it.

See ARRAS SETTING.

cyclorama knuckle. The hardware used to attach the arms of the cyc (cyclorama) bar to a regular pipe. It's a combination of setting rings and a T-shaped connection.

dadaism. An artistic-philosophical movement of the early twentieth century that favored disruption and unlikely combinations. Principal spokesman was Tristan Tzara of Switzerland who wrote *Le Coeur à Gas.* Other plays were Oskar Koloschka's *Sphinx* and *Strohmann,* and Ribemont Dessaignes' *L'Empereur de Chine.* Dadaism developed into surrealism by 1924, and is also an ancestor of the theatre of cruelty and the theatre of the absurd. Its influence can be seen in the mixed-media happenings of the 1960s. The term derives from the French *dada,* meaning "hobbyhorse" and was chosen at random from a dictionary.

See ABSURD THEATRE OF, CRUELTY THEATRE OF, HAPPENING.

dame. A female character in English pantomime that is traditionally played by a man, for example, Jack's mother in *Jack and the Beanstalk* and the stepsisters in *Cinderella.*

See PANTOMINE, PANTS PART.

dance captain. The leader of the chorus in a musical show, also responsible for teaching steps to the dancers after the choreographer has demonstrated them.

See CHORUS.

dark house. A theatre that is no longer used, or a theatre in which there is no performance on the "dark" night, or one in which there is no show currently running.

deck. The stage floor.

declaim. To act using broad gestures and overly dramatic line readings. The style probably developed in sixteenth-century French theatre because of the long, narrow playhouses (many had been built on tennis courts) that had poor acoustics and bad sight lines. The actors resorted to exaggerated techniques to reach the audience. Much melodrama continues to use the same declamatory style, even when not needed. Most modern acting is considerably more restrained.

See CHEW THE SCENERY, HAM, HISTRIONICS, MELODRAMA.

decor. The "look" of the play, including the costumes, set, furnishings, and props. The decor contributes to the play by establishing time periods, elements of characterization, mood, atmosphere, and even, through symbolism, the theme.

See COSTUME, SET, PROPS.

decorum. From the Latin *decorus* for "fitting," a manner appropriate to the time, place, and characters of the play. This includes the way of walking, sitting, talking, gesturing, and dressing. An actor playing a poverty-stricken artist would not have an elegant apartment or expensive clothes. An actor playing a timid Victorian servingmaid would not stride on stage swinging her hips and smirking. An actor playing an illiterate beggar would not speak with a refined accent and the vocabulary of a professor. In criticism the term denotes fidelity to the demands of the genre, for example, neoclassical critics have complained that Shakespeare mixed verse and prose in the speech of a single character, rather than using prose for the lower class and reserving verse for the upper-class characters.

See ANACHRONISM, CRITICISM.

denouement. The solution to the conflict in a play, the untangling of the complications, the answer to the mystery, and the clearing up of the final details. From the French, "untying of the knot." In Euripides' *Medea,* the denouement includes Jason's realization that Medea has killed his sons. He cries out to the gods to witness her cruelty; Medea is carried away in the chariot of the sun god, and the chorus is left to comment that what happens is the will of the gods and beyond mortal understanding. In Alan Ayckbourn's *Absurd Person Singular,* Sidney, who begins the play as subservient to most of the other characters, rises to a position of economic superiority to them. At the climax, he and his wife crash the small party of the others, and in the denouement he insists on involving everyone in a demeaning game of musical chairs—with very unpleasant forfeits and Sidney as the taskmaster. We see in this embarrassing spectacle how life is going to be for all of them from then on.

See ANTICLIMAX, RESOLUTION.

detail scenery. Small, easily changed pieces of scenery in a larger formal setting, or placed in front of the setting and removed at a scene or act change, for example, a desk to suggest a study replaced by a tea table to suggest a drawing room—both with the same background scenery.

See MINIMAL SETTING, SET.

deus ex machina. Literally "the god from the machine." In Greek classical drama, an actual machine—a crane—lowered the actor playing the god into the center of the action so that he or she could unravel the plot complications and direct the denouement. Now the term more often denotes a play that uses a trick ending to extricate the actors from impossible situations; for example, a character awakens to find the whole thing has been a dream, or to find that a long-lost or unheard-of relative has left a fortune. The term can also indicate a character who provides the information that solves the central mystery, as Rosalind in Shakespeare's *As You Like It,* who solves all the romantic tangles by abandoning her disguise of man's clothing, or a character who has the power to right wrongs, as the king in *Tartuffe,* who intervenes and has Tartuffe taken off to prison.

See CLASSICAL DRAMA, DENOUEMENT.

deuteragonist. The second character added to Greek classical drama. Previous to that, there were only the chorus and protagonist. The addition made possible dialog with the protagonist and so sometimes the deuteragonist is considered the foil or the confidant of the protagonist, for example, Horatio to Hamlet.

See CONFIDANT, FOIL.

development. The phase in the action after the exposition has been presented and the entanglements of the plot begin building to the climax. In Oliver Goldsmith's *She Stoops to Conquer,* the point when Marlow and Hastings have been welcomed at Hardcastle Manor and begin treating Squire Hardcastle and his daughter Kate as landlord and maidservant.

See EXPOSITION, RISING ACTION.

dialog. Speech between two or more characters. Dialog in plays provides exposition, carries the plot forward, and helps to define character.

See BOOK, DECORUM, DICTION.

diction. The fourth of Aristotle's Six Elements of Drama, it means both the word choices made by the playwright and the enunciation of the actors delivering the lines.

didactic. An intention to preach or to teach; plays that have as their primary intention the teaching of a lesson or preaching of some belief, for example, the Gerome Ragni–James Rado protest play *Hair,* which condemns all that is wrong with the establishment and promotes the antiestablishment.

See AGITPROP, ALIENATION EFFECT, CHURCH DRAMA.

dimmer. An electronic device to lower or raise the intensity of a stage light. The dimmer, or control, board is a panel of dimmers, each attached to a different piece of lighting equipment. The operator of the board can thus control the intensity and distribution of all the stage lighting from one place.

See LIGHTING PLOT.

dinner theatre. An evening's entertainment, provided by a restaurant or nightclub, consisting of a meal and a performance of an abbreviated version of a play—often starring a famous actor. Murder mysteries and scaled-down versions of musicals are especially popular in dinner theatre.

See CABARET.

dionysian. The opposite principle to Apollonian, that is, the creative, the imaginative, the spontaneous in art. Named for Dionysus, the Greek god of wine and fertility, whose festival, celebrated with drunkenness and licentiousness, is considered by many to be the birth of the drama.

See APOLLONIAN, NEOCLASSICISM, ROMANTICISM.

direct address. Speech directed to the audience. Examples include Launce's complaints about his dog Crab in Shakespeare's *Two Gentlemen of Verona,* Frank's comments on the events of his growing up during World War II in Peter Nichols' *Forget-Me-Not Lane,* and Gallimard's plans to approach the "actress" from the Beijing Opera and his comments on "her" rejection of him in David Henry Hwang's *M. Butterfly.*

See CHORUS CHARACTER, PRESENTATIONAL.

director. The person responsible for the direction of the actors in a play, that is, the one who determines such matters as the tempo and interpretation. The director supervises the players as they rehearse the piece and coordinates all the technical elements that support the performance. In Britain, sometimes called the producer. Many directors have imposed their stamp on a play to such an extent that subsequent productions are strongly influenced. Anton Chekhov called his *Cherry Orchard* a comedy, but Stanislavski directed it as a tragedy, and so have most directors since then. Tennessee Williams has said that his *Streetcar Named Desire* was intended to be "Blanche's play," but in directing it Elia Kazan made it "Stanley's play" and it continues to be presented that way.

See INTERPRETATION, TEMPO.

director's notes. The comments and criticisms the director presents to the cast after a performance. They include all the things the actors need to work on in the next performance as well as praise for things done well. Some directors prefer to give notes after a rehearsal and others find it more beneficial to interrupt the actors to correct or discuss a problem at the moment it becomes evident.

disappearance trap. A trapdoor with an elevator to facilitate quick exits or disappearing tricks onstage.

See CELLAR.

disguise. To wear masks, false hair, character makeup, or clothing either to conceal an actor's identity or to allow him or her to pose as another person. This makes possible anything from complicating the plot to having one actor double in other roles. Before the Restoration in England, women did not act on the stage, so it was a favorite device of playwrights to have the woman character, played by a man, disguise "herself" as a man. Shakespeare does this with Rosalind in *As You Like It,* Viola in *Twelfth Night,* and Julia in *Two Gentlemen of Verona.* In Ferenc Molnar's *The Guardsman,* Nandor disguises himself in order to test his wife's fidelity. Another example is the Phantom of the Opera who disguises himself with a mask in the Andrew Lloyd Webber–Richard Stilgoe production.

See DOUBLING.

dithyramb. A hymn to Dionysus, sung by a chorus of fifty men representing satyrs. The hymn concerned some episode from the life of Dionysus, and at some point the leader of the chorus stepped out and became a soloist—the protagonist—and the resulting dialog became the first drama.

See CHORUS, PROTAGONIST, TRAGEDY.

documentary. A stage production consisting of quick, short scenes depicting current events or problems of modern life, and suggestions for coping with them. Used for educational and propagandistic purposes, for example, in John Dos Passos' *U.S.A.* and Joan Littlewood's *Oh What a Lovely War!*

See LIVING NEWSPAPER, PROPAGANDA PLAY.

dolly. A wagon for shifting scenery; also a cart for moving heavy objects.

See BOAT TRUCK.

domestic tragedy. A play of a tragic nature that deals with the domestic life of ordinary people, as opposed to classical tragedy, which deals with the lives of kings who fall from high estate. Early examples are Thomas Kyd's *Arden of Feversham* and Thomas Heywood's *A Woman Killed with Kindness.* More recent examples are Arthur Miller's *All My Sons* and Elmer Rice's *Street Scene.*

See BOURGEOIS DRAMA.

donkey. An electric winch, used to lift a battened line set attached to a unit of scenery.

See BATTEN.

double casting. The practice of casting two actors or sets of actors who then alternate in performances of a role. This is often done in academic theatre to give more students a chance to participate, or with young children to avoid fatigue. For example, the role of Clara, the little girl in *The Nutcracker,* is usually double cast.

double take. To look and seem not to see anything out of the ordinary and then look again with enhanced recognition and surprise, usually used for comic effect.

doubling. The playing of more than one character in a play by the same actor. If there is some mystery attached, or if the audience is not meant to know of the doubling, the actor is usually referred to in the program as George (Georgina) Spelvin in his or her second role. An example of this practice is the concierge in Ferenc Molnar's *The Guardsman.* In Anthony Shaffer's *Sleuth* several aliases are used in the cast list to preserve the play's central mystery.

See GEORGE SPELVIN.

douser. A mechanical means of extinguishing a stage light; a switch on a dimmer board.

See DIMMER, LIGHTING PLOT.

downstage. In a proscenium arch or thrust stage, that part of the stage closest to the audience. Called "down" from the days when the stage was raked and downstage was literally a few degrees lower than upstage. Used in stage directions to indicate where an actor should stand.

See RAKE.

drag. Slang for woman's apparel when worn by a male actor. To "appear in drag" is to wear such apparel, as do Babberley in Brandon Thomas's *Charley's Aunt* and the two musicians fleeing gangsters in Peter Stone's *Sugar.*

See DISGUISE.

drama. Literature written in dialog form and intended for the theatre. Although plays can be read for enjoyment and instruction, they come most alive when acted on stage. The four main types are tragedy, melodrama, comedy, and farce, although the term *drama* also refers to any serious, as opposed to humorous, play.

See ARISTOTLE'S SIX ELEMENTS OF DRAMA, COMEDY, FARCE, MELODRAMA, TRAGEDY.

dramatic irony. The form of irony in which the audience knows something a character in the play does not. Thus, when Oedipus Rex says he will punish the killer of the king, the audience knows that the killer is Oedipus himself. The irony resides in the contrast between what the speaker intends or expects and what the audience knows is true and will happen.

See EXPOSITION.

dramatic time. The period of time that elapses in the action of the play, as opposed to the actual time it takes the show to run. This may be anything from a few minutes as the same events are shown repeatedly from different characters' points of view—for example, in Tom Stoppard's *Hapgood*—to decades as in Thornton Wilder's *The Long Christmas Dinner,* which covers ninety years of family dinners in a single act.

See CONVENTION.

dramatis personae. From the Latin, meaning the characters in a play; also, the list of them. Shown at the beginning of a play script or in the printed program for a performance, the list may merely give the names of the characters and the actors who play them or may include brief descriptions of the characters. The term is also used in a joking way for the participants in any event.

See CAST.

dramaturg. One who studies a play to interpret it for a company of actors, answering questions about the text, the language, the period, the manners and mores of the characters, the clothing, and the customs. He or she may share in selecting plays, their revisions, or adaptations; choosing translations; writing program notes; and advising technicians. Diana Maddox at the Old Globe Theatre in San Diego, California, is a respected dramaturg, and has contributed to the authenticity of the production of Shakespeare plays presented there.

See CRITICISM, DECORUM.

dramaturgy. The study and interpretation of plays with special attention to the difficulties plays from another period present for the acting company of today. The University of Michigan, among others, offers a doctoral program in dramaturgy.

See CRITICISM, DECORUM.

drame. A play that mixes comedy and tragedy, developed in eighteenth-century France where Denis Diderot was a practitioner. Although such plays were serious in nature, they often ended happily. Today they are more often called tragicomedy or dragedy.

See DOMESTIC TRAGEDY.

drawing room comedy. So called because the action takes place in the drawing room of upper-class characters.

See COMEDY OF MANNERS.

draw line. The operating line of a traveling curtain rigging. The two halves of a curtain are hung from two overlapping sections of track. Carriers are attached to the top of the curtain at twelve-inch intervals. The draw line (rope) is attached to the first of these carriers, which pulls the rest of the carriers to open or close the curtain.

See CURTAIN, STAGE CREW.

dream play. A fantasy drama that resembles a dream because of its hazy atmosphere, nonrealistic flow of events one into another, or disconnected series of scenes. The term comes from August Strindberg's *The Dream Play,* in which he intended to show the viewpoint of a dreamer by destroying limitations of time, place, and logical sequence.

See LINEAR PLOT.

dresser. One who assists an actor by laying out costumes and makeup, and assisting with changing and hairdressing. Generally hired and paid by the individual actor.

dressing the house. The practice of scattering a small audience throughout the house, leaving pairs of seats vacant here and there, rather than full rows or sections. This gives the impression of a larger audience than is actually present.

See PAPERING THE HOUSE.

dressing the stage. Loosely used to mean decorating the set. As a stage direction, it means moving the actors into a better balance to avoid grouping in one place or in a straight line.

dress parade. A wardrobe check during which the actors wear their various costume changes through a kind of parade that enables the director and costumer to check on the effect of the colors under lighting, the fit and suitability of each costume, and the compatibility with other costumes in the same scene as well as with the movement required of the actor in the costume. This generally occurs at least a week before dress rehearsal.

See COSTUME, WARDROBE MISTRESS.

dress rehearsal. The last rehearsal before a play is performed before an audience, usually held the night before the opening. Treated as a performance, it is done in full costume, with full technical effects, and played straight through without stopping for any miscues or mistakes.

droll. Short, comic sketch extracted or altered from a longer play and performed, probably surreptitiously, during Oliver Cromwell's Commonwealth in seventeenth-century England. The word comes from *drolleries* and is also used to designate the actors who play in such scenes or take other humorous parts. Two famous drolls are the artisans' rehearsal of Pyramus and Thisbe in Shakespeare's *A Midsummer Night's Dream* and the grave diggers' scene in *Hamlet.* Such shows usually ended with a lively jig or dance.

See BURLESQUE, CLOWN CHARACTER.

drop. A large piece of canvas mounted at the rear of the stage and long enough to reach the floor, painted with a scene and serving as a background to the action. It may have battens at the top and bottom, or be framed on all four sides.

See BACKDROP.

drum and shaft. An early system of moving scenery, using a rope attached to a cylindrical shaft that is turned by a lever.

See BARREL SYSTEM.

dumb show. A story conveyed entirely through gestures; also, pantomime, though *dumb show* is often reserved for the show-within-a-show;

for example, when the players in Shakespeare's *Hamlet* silently reenact a murder that parallels that of King Hamlet. Also, the pageant staged by Prospero for Miranda's marriage in Shakespeare's *The Tempest*. The form was especially popular during the sixteenth and seventeenth centuries in England.

See PANTOMIME.

duodrama. An entertainment in which two actors present a short piece in front of a chorus of silent figures who dance or move about to express what is being said. It was often used to fill out a program in the eighteenth-century theatre.

duolog. A complete work in which there are just two characters. There are many modern examples: the two diplomats of Lee Blessing's *A Walk in the Woods;* Jessie and her mother in Marsha Norman's *'Night, Mother;* and the two mountain climbers in Patrick Meyer's *K 2*.

dutchman. A strip of canvas glued over the crack between two flats. The strip is painted to match the flats and provides a seamless set. "To dutch" is to apply the strip to the flats.

dynamic character. One who grows and changes throughout the play rather than remaining static. Most protagonists undergo such change, unless it is the point of the playwright that there has been no growth. Examples include Tracey Lord in Phillip Barry's *The Philadelphia Story* who learns to be more accepting of herself and others; Heidi Holland in Wendy Wasserstein's *The Heidi Chronicles* who learns to stop blaming herself for not "having it all;" and the father in Pierre Corneille's *The Illusion* who journeys to find his son and grows to understand their relationship.

See STATIC CHARACTERS.

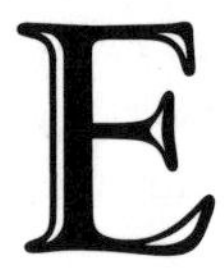

ecclesiastical drama. Plays based on the liturgy of the Christian church and performed throughout Europe in the Middle Ages. Originally performed in the church itself to act out Gospel stories for the mostly illiterate congregation, these plays were eventually moved to the church steps and then into the town square. The most famous sequence presented was the "Quem Quaeritis?" (Whom do you seek?), which followed the Gospel account of the meeting between the angel at the tomb and the three Marys on Easter morning.

See CARNIVAL MASS, CORPUS CHRISTI PLAYS, CYCLE PLAYS, MYSTERY PLAY.

economy of roles. The limitation on the number of actors in the performance of Greek classical drama. By Sophocles' time, three were used, each of whom might take several roles. This was, of course, in addition to the chorus members.

See CLASSICAL DRAMA, PROTAGONIST, DEUTERAGONIST.

educational theatre. Theatre conducted in or as an adjunct to schools. Also, theatre with a didactic purpose.

See ACADEMIC THEATRE, DIDACTIC.

effects. Onstage and offstage sounds, made by a sound effects technician or, more commonly today, by prerecorded tapes. Also, patterns and shadowing created by lighting.

See CHIAROSCURO, CRASH BOX.

ekkyklema. Also spelled eccyclema. In Greek classical drama probably a moveable platform, or merely a wheeled couch carrying an actor or actors, and depicting the results of some offstage event, for example, Clytemnestra standing over the body of the murdered Agamemnon in Aeschylus' *Agamemnon.*

emotional recall. An acting technique using some personal experience to trigger emotion in a scene onstage.

See AFFECTIVE MEMORY, METHOD ACTING, SENSE MEMORY, STANISLAVSKY METHOD.

empathy. The act of an audience's identifying with the characters in a play. Empathy goes beyond mere sympathy to the point of causing an audience to flinch when a character is struck or to have a racing heartbeat when a character is in danger.

See CATHARSIS.

ensemble playing. The type of acting in which a cast works as a team to create a total effect rather than a group of individual performances. A play such as Anton Chekhov's *Uncle Vanya,* written as an ensemble piece, may have some roles with more lines than others, but all the characters have equal importance in the total production.

See STAR TURN.

entr'acte. Musical interlude between the acts of a play, for example, the olio numbers between the acts of a melodrama. Such interludes have been largely eliminated by the trend toward greater realism in drama and the desire not to distract attention from the play.

See OLIO.

entrance. The act of entering onto the acting area during a performance. Also, any opening in the set through which an actor can enter. In the early seventeenth-century French theatre, there was a convention of *decor simutanee* (simultaneous settings) that permitted several different entrances onto the stage, each depicting a different place. When an actor entered by a given opening, it indicated to the audience that he or she was in that locale.

epic theatre. A movement in the German theatre of the 1920s that asserted that the appeal of theatre should be to the intellect of the audience rather than to its emotions. Bertolt Brecht was the leading exponent.

See DIDACTIC.

epigram. A short, polished, witty, often satirical comment. Oscar Wilde is known for his epigrammatic style, and *The Importance of Being Earnest* is filled with examples:

> ALGERNON: More than half of modern culture depends on what one shouldn't read.
>
> JOHN: When in town one amuses oneself. When in the country one amuses other people.

See COMEDY OF MANNERS, DRAWING ROOM COMEDY.

epilog. A speech made to conclude a play or given outside the final action of the play, as when Lady Teazle in Richard Sheridan's *The School for Scandal* steps forward to bid her farewell to all the pleasures of the town as she must retire to the country, or when Prospero in Shakespeare's *The Tempest* gives up his magic powers and calls on the audience to release the actors with applause.

episode. In Greek classical drama the sections of action and dialog that alternate with the choral odes. Today the term can mean anything from an incident to a whole scene. In Henrik Ibsen's *The Wild Duck,* Gregers is shown the attic setting where Hedvig keeps the wild duck as a pet. This little episode is complete in itself, but it also serves the play by foreshadowing the ending.

See ACTION, CLASSICAL DRAMA.

epode. In Greek classical drama the third and last part of a choral ode.

See ANTISTROPHE, STROPHE.

equity waiver house. In California a theatre with fewer than one hundred seats in which an equity member, with permission, may work without receiving minimum wage. This is done to enable professional actors to guest in community productions or participate in showcases for agents and producers. Also called "ninety-nine seat house."

See ACTORS' EQUITY.

ERF. Abbreviation for *e*llipsoidal *r*eflector *f*loodlight, a device for throwing a broad wash of light over a wide area without having a sharp edge to the beam. A single ERF can light a window backing and a bank of ERFs can light a cyclorama.

See LIGHTING PLOT.

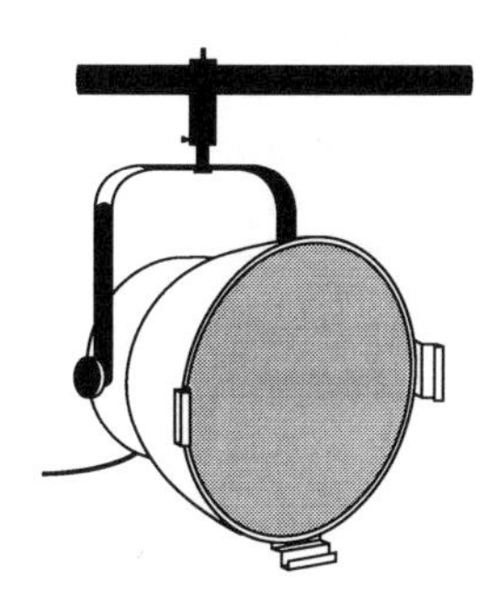
Ellipsoidal Reflector Floodlight

erudite theatre. A type of theatre that caters to a certain class of people and concerns itself with recreating a former style or movement in the drama, for example, The Melodrama in Pismo Beach, California, and the Oregon Shakespeare Festival Theatre in Ashland.

existentialism. A modern philosophy strongly affecting the theatre of the absurd, which depicts humanity as insecure in an irrational universe. Jean-Paul Sartre's *No Exit* presents three people locked into a situation from which there is no escape and who eventually realize that "hell is other people."

See ABSURD, THEATRE OF.

exit. The leaving of the acting area by an actor. Also, the way by which he or she leaves.

exodos. In Greek classical tragedy the last action of the play after the final choral ode; also used to describe the exiting of the chorus as they sing that final ode. In Sophocles' *Electra* all but the leader exit, the doors open to show "the living and the dead," and then the leader speaks the last lines of the play.

See CHORUS.

exposition. Information about what has happened before the play opens. Some of this is provided in program notes, but most must come through the dialog of the actors. Often, exposition is provided by servants who talk about their masters, as in the opening of Shakespeare's *Romeo and Juliet,* or by chorus characters, such as the Priestess of Apollo in Aeschylus' *Eumenides,* who tells the whole story of Orestes, or by the protagonist, as in Georgina's opening monolog in Elmer Rice's *Dream Girl.* As Georgina dresses for the day, we hear about her dreams, hopes, and aspirations as well as the stumbling blocks to them.

See ACTION.

expressionism. An offshoot of impressionism that intends to show the inner psychological reality of its characters. One technique used to achieve this is an externalization of the internal emotions of a character. For example, when Mr. Zero in Elmer Rice's *The Adding Machine* is fired from his job, the section of the set on which he is standing spins around to suggest his bewilderment. Scenery and lighting are often used to distort the normal and create a dreamlike atmosphere. In Georg Kaiser's *From Morn to Midnight,* most of the characters were dressed the same to emphasize the uniformity of modern life.

See DREAM PLAY, IMPRESSIONISM.

extravaganza. An elaborate, lavish, spectacular production, usually musical, with a large cast, expensive costumes, and grand sets, and intended solely for entertainment. It may have elements of fantasy as well. The *Ziegfeld Follies* and *Earl Carroll's Vanities* were long-running extravaganzas that set the style for the genre.

See BURLESQUE, REVUE.

extrinsic idea. The idea(s) the play expresses on its literal level. It is often verbalized by a character or the chorus. In Lorraine Hansberry's *A Raisin in the Sun,* Lena remarks, "Seem like God didn't see fit to give the black man nothing but dreams—but He did give us children to make them dreams seem worthwhile." She is quoting her late husband and the words strongly affect her son and move him to a course of action.

See PLAYWRIGHT'S VOICE.

eyeball strip. A line of swivel-mounted, parabolic spotlight reflector lamps, used for selective focusing. This is an improvement over the older open trough, because each light can have its own built-in reflector and gel holder. So called because of the eyeball shape of the pars.

See GEL, PAR, SPOTLIGHT.

fabula atellana. From *fabula,* meaning "a play," and Atella, a town in southern Italy; a second-century B.C. farce, improvised with stock characters and presented on market days. During the first century B.C., some were written down by Pomponius and Novius and used as curtain raisers. Surviving titles include *The Farmer, The Vine-Gatherers,* and *The Woodpile.* This form is the ancestor of the commedia dell'arte.

See COMMEDIA DELL'ARTE, CURTAIN RAISER, FARCE, IMPROVISATION, STOCK CHARACTERS.

fabula palliata. A play translated into Latin from Greek New Comedy. It is named for the *pallium,* a Greek cloak. Terence was a leading writer of such plays and his six surviving plays are based on Greek comedies. For example, *The Self Tormentor* is based on a play of the same name by Menander.

See CONTAMINATION, NEW COMEDY.

fabula praetexta. An original play in Latin based on Roman legend or a historical event. It is named for the *toga praetexta,* the purple outer garment worn by high public officials of Rome. Naevius and Ennius were writers of this form, but the only existing play is *Octavia,* whose author is unknown, about the wife of the emperor Nero.

fabula togata. A Roman comedy, popular from about 150 to 50 B.C., having nationalistic themes and a realistic presentation. The scenes were laid in small towns and the characters taken from the middle or lower classes. Some seventy titles are known, including *Divorce, Letter,* and *The Stepson* by the chief writer of the form, Afranius.

fade. A gradual dimming of the intensity of the stage lighting. This is done by slowly turning the major control knob at the control board or by manually pushing down the row of lighting control levers. The fade is often used at the end of a scene when the director wants to give the audience a moment to dwell on what it has just seen or heard.

See BLACKOUT.

falling action. The action after the climax of the plot. There is a lessening of the tension and the action proceeds to the denouement, or resolution. For example, in John Millington Synge's *In the Shadow of the Glen,* the climax occurs when Nora bundles a few belongings into her shawl, and we know that she has decided to leave with the tramp. The tramp's subsequent recitation of the beauties of the road, and Nora's grumbling at its probable discomforts, do nothing to change the decision implied by the packing of her belongings. They only serve as the falling action, as do the toasting and drinking by Dan and Micheal that follow the exit of Nora and the tramp.

See CLIMAX, RISING ACTION.

farce. From the French, meaning "to stuff." Farce is an extreme form of comedy that depends on quick tempo and flawless timing by the actors. Since farce is "stuffed" with improbable events and farfetched coincidences, the audience must not be allowed time to think things through.

Farce dates to the satyr plays of Greek drama and was seen in the *fabula atellana* of the Roman empire, in the commedia, in such early English comedies as *Ralph Roister Doister,* in the plays of Molière, in the Victorian dramas of Brandon Thomas and Arthur Pinero, and, currently, in the bedroom farces of Brian Rix and Ray Cooney. Thornton Wilder's *The Matchmaker,* with its young provincials on the loose in New York City, is a fine example of the boisterous, exuberant manner of the farce.

See ALDWYCH FARCE, COMEDY, FABULA ATELLANA, SATYR PLAY, WHITEHALL FARCE.

feed line. A line delivered by the straight man or woman in a comic situation. The whole purpose is to enable the comedian to deliver the punch line or funny remark. In Neil Simon's *The Odd Couple,* Felix is complaining about Oscar's late arrival home. Oscar replies that he couldn't get a cab—the feed line—and Felix snaps, "Since when do they have cabs in Hannigan's bar?"

fescennine verses. An early Italian preliterary form of rude banter by masked actors. Such verses originated in the town of Fescennine in central Italy and were usually performed at festivals and weddings, the latter occasion often prompting ribald jesting.

FEV. An acronym for *F*rench *e*namel *v*arnish. FEV is often recommended in older books of stagecraft for scenery painting, but it has been supplanted by easier-to-use water-based products.

fill light. A soft light or wash that comes from the opposite direction of the key light and provides a difference in intensity or color from the accent of the key light on an actor's face.

See KEY LIGHT, WASH.

flashback. In a nonlinear plot, the return to a previous event or events. A **flashforward** would take the actors into some future event. Both are used in stage adaptations of Charles Dickens's *A Christmas Carol*—Scrooge is taken to Christmas Past and then to Christmas Future. The flashback is also used by Arthur Laurents in *A Clearing in the Woods,* when Virginia, who has loved and lost Andy, forms a magic circle with him to shut out the mistakes of the past and to find the day two years before when things began to go wrong so that she can change what happened and win him back. Arnold Wesker's *Their Very Own and Golden City* uses a flashforward to show what the future holds for the play's characters, and South African Mbongeni Ngema's *Township Fever* uses narration with flashbacks to tell the story.

See LINEAR PLOT.

flat. The basic unit of stage scenery. It usually consists of a wooden frame with canvas or muslin stretched to fill it, and a wooden crosspiece for backing. Several flats lashed or cleated together form a set. Flats are also used to mask offstage areas that are glimpsed by the audience through a set's windows or when a door is opened onstage.

See SCENERY.

flies. The area above the stage, hidden from the audience by a border or drapery, to which scenery can be lifted clear of the stage. Also called the fly loft. Many modern theatres don't have such a space above the stage, and so are restricted to plays with a single set, minimal settings, or other conventional staging.
See CATWALK, GRID.

flipper. A jog, or narrow flat, usually made of plywood, hinged to a standard flat to help support the flat as it stands alone.
See FLAT, JOG.

float down. A term used to describe the sailing, kitelike motion of a flat when it is allowed to fall from the flies.
See FLIES.

flood. Used as a shortened term for *floodlight.* The term also refers to the widespread focus on a spotlight having the effect of flooding the stage with light.

floodlight. A light with a large reflector and a high-wattage lamp that produces a broad fill of light on the stage. Its beam is not easily controlled, but the light spreads illumination evenly.

floor plan. Also called the ground plan, it is an overhead drawing to scale that shows the outline of the set with the location of entrances, furniture, and props.

fluffed line. A mishandled line of dialog—that is, a line not said at all, one that has been muddled ("you gold oat" for "you old goat") or one that is delivered in the wrong place.
See GOES UP.

fly(ing). To fly scenery is to hoist it to or from the flies. The term may also apply to the flying of an actor on wires across the stage, as, for example, Peter Pan and the children in James M. Barrie's *Peter Pan* and Puck in Shakespeare's *A Midsummer Night's Dream.*
See FLIES, GRID, STAGE CREW.

focus. The adjustment of the size and shape of a beam from a stage light; also, the direction in which the beam is aimed. In addition, actors use the term to describe the act of concentrating or staying in character throughout all lines, and stage business. The terms "taking focus" and "giving focus" are used by directors to indicate how an actor takes the attention of the audience from another actor or relinquishes it.

See CONCENTRATION, IN THE MOMENT.

foil. A character in a play so different from another in personality or appearance that he or she highlights the other by contrast. For instance, a tall, handsome, socially adept protagonist may have as his buddy a short, comical-looking bumbler. The bumbler serves as the foil. Many famous comedy teams are like this: Abbott and Costello, Martin and Lewis, Laurel and Hardy. In Ferenc Molnár's *Liliom,* Marie, a little country mouse of a girl, is a foil for her friend Julie who, after a year in Budapest, considers herself quite a sophisticate. In Beth Henley's *Abundance,* Bess and Macon have both come to the Wyoming Territory in the 1860s as mail-order brides, but Macon has vision and dreams, and Bess is ready to settle for whatever she gets.

See CONFIDANT(E).

folio. From the Latin *folium,* meaning a "leaf." The term refers to a sheet of paper folded in half to form four pages and also to a volume made up of such sheets—for example, Shakespeare's First Folio (1623). Currently, *folio* is used in printing and publishing to mean "a page number."

follow cue. A lighting direction that comes so close to another lighting direction that it doesn't need a separate number on the cue sheet of the lighting technician.

See LIGHTING PLOT.

fool. A licensed jester at court and the comic characters based on him, such as Shakespeare's fools Feste, Touchstone, and Costard. Often dressed in motley, fools commented ironically on the action in a play. Also the character of the "wise fool" who, seemingly simpleminded or slow-witted, expresses real insight into what is going on. For example, Elwood P. Dowd in Mary Chase's *Harvey* displays more good sense than his relatives who want to institutionalize him.

See CLOWN CHARACTER, MOTLEY.

foot candle. A unit of light measurement. One foot candle is the amount of light that falls on a surface located one foot away from a candle.

foreshadow. To give the audience clues about an upcoming event in the play. The early appearance of the blind Tiresias in *Oedipus Rex,* for instance, foreshadows the later appearance of the blind Oedipus. Foreshadowing is used with great effect not only in Greek tragedy but also in murder mysteries like Agatha Cristie's *The Mouse Trap* and realistic dramas like Anton Chekhov's *The Seagull.* The technique creates interest and arouses suspense. It also prepares an audience for a climactic event.

See COMPLICATION.

forestage. The space in front of the curtain line, also called the apron.

form. The structure of a literary work, as distinguished from its content. In drama the form is acts, divided into scenes, divided into speeches. The term is also used to distinguish the elements that make one genre different from another. In that sense, drama may be subdivided into tragedy, comedy, farce, and melodrama, and the elements of each may be explored further.

See CRITICISM.

found space. Not a conventional theatre, or even a multipurpose room used for performances, but any area a group of actors finds available and uses to stage a play. Examples include a garage, cafeteria, sports stadium, private living room, parking lot, or lecture hall (the raked seating works well for the audience).

See ACTING AREA.

fourth wall. The invisible wall of a set through which the audience sees the action of a play. In representational performances, the wall is intact even to the extent of an actor looking out a "window" in that wall or examining a picture "hung" there. In presentational performances, an actor may "break" the fourth wall by addressing the audience or going out among them. In the Fran Charnos revue *The All Night Strut,* cast members go into the audience and bring people onto the stage to dance with them.

See PRESENTATIONAL, REPRESENTATIONAL.

freeze. To remain motionless onstage for a predetermined number of beats, especially for a laugh after a funny line, or in tableau fashion as the curtain descends or for a blackout.

See CURTAIN LINE, TAKE.

Fresnel (fr'nél). A spotlight with a stepped lens of concentric rings. Named for its inventor, a Fresnel casts a pool of light with soft edges that blends with other lights. It is a favorite of small touring companies and students because it mounts easily on portable light trees (arrangements of pipes, quickly assembled) and can be used in anything from an auditorium to a found space.

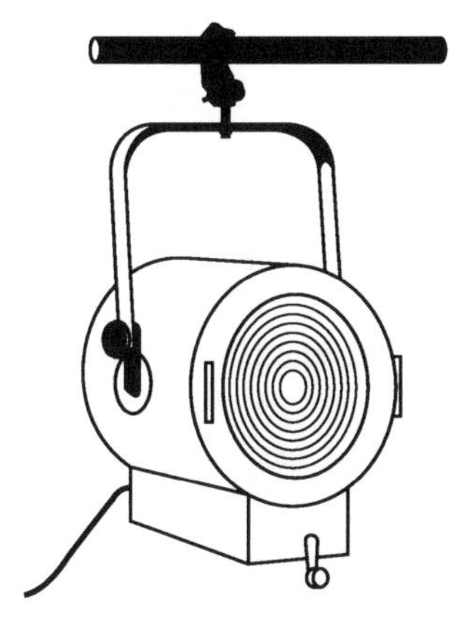

Fresnel spotlight

fringe theatre. Productions that are often experimental and frequently based on nontraditional themes, and that tend away from realism and toward a frank theatricalism. Also known as Off Broadway and Off-Off Broadway, and, in England, as lunchtime theatre and café theatre. In Scotland the Edinburgh Festival originally developed small presentations on its fringe area that have come to rival the main festival. Writers and their works that began in fringe theatres include Sam Shepard, *The Tooth of the Crime;* Rochelle Owens, *Futz;* Terrence McNally, *Next;* Lanford Wilson, *The Rimers of Eldritch;* LeRoi Jones (now Imamu Amiri Baraka), *Dutchman;* Lonne Elder III, *Ceremonies in Dark Old Men;* and Ed Bullins, *A Son Come Home. Theatre Weekly* lists over one hundred fringe theatres currently operating in New York City.

See BROADWAY, OFF-BROADWAY.

front lighting. Lighting that comes from the house and shines onto the stage. This may be from banks of lights placed just in front of the forestage, or follow-spots.

front of the house. Those parts of the theatre used by the audience, as distinct from those used by the actors; generally, the house side of the

fourth wall. This includes the seating, lobby, ticket booth, foyer, bar, and terrace, and is the responsibility of house management.
See HOUSE, HOUSE MANAGER.

full scenery. A box set of strictly representational style that imitates its original in life. It contrasts to fragmentary scenery that may use an archway to suggest a door or a suspended frame to suggest a painting.
See SET(TING).

funnel. A shield of sheet metal from one to three feet long fastened to the front of a spotlight to absorb and control any stray light that might fall outside the area to be illuminated. Also known as a high hat or a top hat.
See SPOTLIGHT.

gamos. Derived from the Greek *gamos,* meaning "marriage," and referring to the romantic endings of "old comedies" of classical drama. After the "happy idea" announced in the prologue has been put into practice in the episodes, the play usually ends with feasting and the marriage of the romantic leads. For example, Aristophanes' *Birds* ends with the wedding feast of Pisthetaerus and Basileia, and then the happy couple fly away to the palace of Zeus where they are to reign.

gel. A very thin sheet of gelatin, available in a wide range of colors, set in a frame, and mounted in front of a light in order to color the beam directed onto the set. Surprise pink, for example, supplies a cheerful look, and moonlight blue, despite its romantic name, tends to muddy the colors of the set and costumes. The sheets of colored plastic now coming into use are also called gels.

genre. A category of composition. In literature, the main categories are poetry, fiction, nonfiction, and drama. Drama is further divided into tragedy, comedy, farce, and melodrama, and each of these may be subdivided by style or content. Comedy, for example, may be absurdist, comedy of humors, comedy of manners, or romantic. Genre studies examine a particular work in relation to others of the same kind, determining how closely it meets the characteristics of that genre.

See CRITICISM.

George Spelvin. False name used in the play program to conceal from the audience that an actor is playing two roles. It is thought to have been used first in the 1907 production of *Brewster's Millions* by Winchell Smith and Frederick Thompson. A director wishing to remain unknown uses Alan Smithee in the program listing.

See DOUBLING.

ghost walks, the. A term used by actors for payday. In Shakespeare's time, the actor playing the Ghost in *Hamlet* was also the stage manager who delivered the pay to each actor in the cast. Thus, when it was payday, the ghost walked among them.

gimmick. A device, bit of stage business, catch phrase, or vocal quirk used to attract and hold the audience's attention. In Arthur Laurents's *Gypsy,* three strippers sing a song to convince neophyte Gypsy Rose Lee that "You Gotta Have a Gimmick" to get noticed on stage. Some performers have become so identified with their gimmicks that audiences expect them in every performance. Al Jolson used to stop the action of his show to sing a new song that had caught his fancy. Bert Lahr used a quavery voice to advantage. Harpo Marx, who could speak, chose not to, and instead used the squeak of a squeeze-bulb horn.

See GESTURE, LAZZO, SHTICK.

gesture. Any movement of shoulder, arm, hand, leg, foot, or head by an actor to convey meaning. For example, an actor shrugs to indicate scorn or lack of knowledge or interest. In Peter Shaffer's *Lettice & Lovage,* Maggie Smith waves a limp hand in airy disdain for tour guides who tell only the unembellished—and to her mind, dull—truth about the house being viewed.

gobo. Also called a "cookie." A disc of heat-resistant material into which a pattern—circles, stars, tree branches—has been cut. When the gobo is placed over the lens of an ellipsoidal spotlight, the pattern is projected onto a backdrop, set wall, or cyclorama.

See MAT, SPOTLIGHT.

god from the machine. The translation of *deus ex machina.* It refers to the device or person used to resolve the action of the play, usually in an artificial manner.
See DEUS EX MACHINA.

goes up. The time a performance begins, referring to a curtain going up, or being raised. The term is also used to designate the day the play opens its run, and it is slang for forgetting one's lines on stage.
See FLUFFED LINE.

grand drape. A very short curtain hanging at the top of the proscenium arch and in front of the main curtain. It serves to decorate and mask the top of the stage.
See MASK, PROSCENIUM ARCH.

greasepaint. A type of stage makeup having a very greasy texture. It is no longer widely used because of its harshness to the complexion, but it is still the best substance for an even and thorough coverage of the skin.

Greek it, to. To use fake lettering in scenic design. The lettering looks like Greek but makes no sense. It may be used as a border to suggest a Greek setting.

green room. A room backstage where actors wait for their entrance cues. The cast may also assemble there after a performance to hear the director's comments. The original room may have been painted green and so set the style, or the term may be a corruption of "scene room," a place where scenery was stored and where actors could wait to go onstage.

grid, gridiron. The framework of wood or steel above the stage from which scenery is hung or flown.
See FLIES.

grip. A member of the stage crew, so called because he or she grips the scenery to move or place it.
See STAGE CREW.

ground cloth. A waterproof canvas covering the whole stage floor. It may be painted to simulate wooden planks or marble, or just a color related to the rest of the set to unify the total picture. Since regular scene paint would easily rub off when walked on, the ground cloth is painted with dyes or, when waterproofing is necessary, with oil paint.

groundling. In Elizabethan times, a spectator who stood in the pit immediately in front of the stage to see a performance. Since these were the cheapest of tickets, those who stood there were often unruly, and so, many low-comedy lines or gestures were thrown their way to keep them entertained.

See PIT.

ground plan. A bird's-eye view of the set. Also called the floor plan.

See FLOOR PLAN.

ground row. Also spelled *groundrow,* the term used to refer to a strip of lights at the foot of a back scene, but now refers to small scenery standing independently onstage, such as a hedge or a riverbank.

guerrilla theatre. From the Spanish, meaning "little war," and parallel to guerrilla warfare since the players seize opportunities of public meetings to stage short, hard-hitting skits on controversial subjects or to call attention to a specific issue. Also called "protest theatre" and staged by groups like El Teatro Campesino in California, which promoted the United Farm Workers' strike.

See AGITPROP, DIDACTIC, PROPAGANDA PLAY.

guilds. In medieval Europe, organizations of people working in the same craft. The guilds were roughly equivalent to later trade unions, but also had the element of shared religious devotion. Guilds often sponsored public performances of mystery plays in their towns, choosing plays that had some relation to their own craft. For example, the bakers might sponsor a play about the harrowing of hell, since their baking pans could be used to create the din needed in the performance.

See MYSTERY PLAY.

gypsy. A member of the chorus, so called because of his or her nomadic existence, moving from show to show or from place to place on the road with a show. Even an established headline performer like dancer-choreographer Gwen Verdon calls herself a gypsy, in recognition of her days in the chorus and her affinity with those performers.

See CHORUS.

halation. An unwanted leaking of light from a spotlight, forming a halo around the light beam.

ham. An actor who overacts, often with elaborate gestures, exaggerated facial expressions, or vocal excesses inappropriate to the play. An actor who attempts to keep the focus on himself or herself by such devices when it should pass to others.

See HISTRIONICS, MUGGING, UPSTAGING.

hamartia. From the Greek, meaning "error" or "sin." According to Aristotle, it is the fatal flaw that causes the downfall of the tragic hero. It may be overweening pride, bad judgment, or simple error. It may be a family trait. In Antigone's refusal to obey the law that forbids the burial of traitors, her pride leads her to assert her beliefs, feeling that she is right and the others are wrong. Her actions express a family trait of impetuosity—she is, after all, the daughter of Oedipus, and his impetuous slaying of his (unrecognized) father set in motion his own downfall.

See HUBRIS.

happening. A type of performance that came to prominence in the late 1950s, but was rooted in the earliest of improvisational theatre. It is present today in many of the elaborate rock concerts staged by groups who depend more on spectacle than on musical ability, and where the audience is as much a participant as a viewer. The happening was a mixed-media presentation, combining elements of script, structured theatre games, music, dance, and improvisation. An example is John Cage's *Sonata Six* in which the participants have certain tasks to complete before the piece is over.

See PARTICIPATORY THEATRE.

Harlequin. The most famous of the commedia dell'arte clown characters. Also known as Arlecchino.

See ARLECCHINO, COMMEDIA DELL'ARTE.

harlequinade. An early eighteenth-century play in which the Harlequin or a similar character stars. The plays involved music, magic, and mime, and the plots revolved around the romantic escapades of Arlecchino and Columbine. By the nineteenth century, the character of Pantaloon (Pantalone) had become the principal figure and his antics eclipsed the lovers. The form was largely forgotten by the twentieth century.

See COMMEDIA DELL'ARTE.

heavy, the. The villain in a play. The villainy may take the form of evil deeds, as when Iago incites Othello to murderous jealousy in Shakespeare's *Othello,* or when Bill Sikes kills the devoted Nancy in Lionel Bart's *Oliver!,* or when Jack Mannering attempts to drive his wife insane in Patrick Hamilton's *Angel Street.* Or it may be that the villain thwarts the protagonist or the young lovers, as does the tyrannical Mr. Barrett in Rudolf Besier's *The Barretts of Wimpole Street.*

See STOCK CHARACTERS.

hero, heroine. The protagonist of the play. If the character is outside conventional morality or behavior, he or she may be called an antihero. The tragic hero is one who falls from a high position because of a tragic flaw.

See PROTAGONIST.

heroic couplet. A pair of rhyming lines of iambic pentameter; the name derives from its use by John Dryden in verse dramas.

See COUPLET.

heroic drama. A kind of tragedy, popular during the Restoration in England, in which larger-than-life characters expressed grand passions and performed spectacular deeds. It did not necessarily end tragically, as the hero often triumphed over the villain, saved the kingdom, and won the fair lady. John Dryden's *The Conquest of Granada* remains the chief example of the genre.

See SATIRE.

high comedy. Sophisticated comedy emphasizing verbal wit more than physical action. It appeals to the intellect and deals with the inconsistencies and incongruities of human nature and the follies of social manners. The comedies of William Wycherley, William Congreve, Oscar Wilde, G. B. Shaw, Noel Coward, Simon Gray, and Alan Aykbourn provide many examples.

See COMEDY OF MANNERS, DRAWING ROOM COMEDY.

history play. A play dealing with a historical subject, such as Shakespeare's *Henry IV* and *Richard II,* and Don Taylor's *The Roses of Eyem,* the true story of the village of Eyem in Derbyshire, England. The village fell victim to the plague of 1665 and elected to seal itself off from the world to stop the spread of the disease. The play begins with the cast of over fifty villagers and ends with the handful who survived.

See CHRONICLE PLAY.

histrionics. Overly dramatic acting, filled with excessive emotion and affectation.

See CHEWING THE SCENERY, HAM, MUGGING.

hit your mark. A direction for an actor to go to a certain place onstage and deliver a line, make an entrance, or perform some stage business.

hokum. A slang expression for gimmicks, tricks, or bits of business used by an actor to get a response, usually laughter, from an audience. The classic is taking or giving a cream pie in the face.

hot spot. An area downstage right that many actors feel is an especially good focal point, because they believe audiences naturally look to that spot.

house. The seating area of a theatre, but also the audience itself, as in the phrase, "That was a tough house tonight."

house curtain. In a proscenium arch theatre, the main curtain that closes off the stage from the view of the audience. It may lower and raise or part in the middle.

See PROSCENIUM ARCH.

house manager, management. One who oversees or runs the box office where reservations are taken and tickets sold. The H.M. is also responsible for getting the audience into and out of the theatre. He or she hires and instructs the ushers and prepares the box office statement at the end of the performance. In small companies and academic theatres, the H.M. may also assume the duties of the publicist, so that he or she supervises all matters relating to the audience.

See FRONT OF THE HOUSE.

house right/left. Directions viewed from the perspective of the audience, as distinguished from the perspective of the actors, which would be stage right and left.

house seats. Seats set aside at each performance to cover any mix-up in tickets or for important guests. If not needed, they are released for sale just before curtain time.

hubris, hybris. From the Greek, meaning "overweening pride." A type of *hamartia,* the tragic flaw that causes the downfall of the hero. In Aeschylus' *The Persians,* King Xerxes is moved by pride to lead his vast army againt the Greeks and is defeated. In the second stasimon, the chorus sings of the humbling of the formerly proud Persians by the power of Zeus. In Shakespeare's *King Lear,* Lear himself is so blinded by his pride that he is unable to appreciate the loyalty and sincerity of his daughter Cordelia, and so falls prey to the ambition of his hypocritical daughters Regan and Goneril. In Arthur Miller's *All My Sons,* Joe Keller's pride in his business and his financial success leads him to sell defective airplane parts. This directly causes the death of pilots fighting in World War II, and indirectly causes the suicide of his beloved son Larry, who has learned of his father's guilt.

See STASIMON.

humors. According to Renaissance medicine, the four primary fluids of the human body—blood, phlegm, choler (yellow bile), and melancholy (black bile)—that were responsible for the human temperament. A preponderance of one of the fluids produced a particular temperament: too much blood made a person sanguine; too much phlegm, phlegmatic; too much yellow bile, choleric; and too much black bile, melancholic. Ben Jonson used the theory in his comedy *Everyman in His Humor.* Each character acted according to his humor; for example, the choleric Knowell and the sanguine Justice Clement. It was believed that a perfect balance of humors resulted in the perfect temperament. The comedy of humors makes use not of rounded characters but of characters with predominant traits, and so owes something to the stock characters of Roman comedy.

See COMEDY, STOCK CHARACTERS.

hypokrites. The Greek word meaning "actor."

I

imagery. Words and phrases in dialog that appeal to any of the five senses or that paint pictures in the mind of the audience. The term is also used to identify figurative language in general—similes, metaphors, and other figures of speech. Imagery may be used by a character to convey vivid pictures. One example is "The Winter's Song," usually sung by Costard as an epilog to Shakespeare's *Love's Labor's Lost:*

> When all aloud the wind doth blow,
> And coughing drowns the parson's saw,
> And birds sit brooding in the snow,
> And Marian's nose looks red and raw, . . .

Critics study patterns of imagery to explore all the meanings in a play. Caroline Spurgeon's *Shakespeare's Imagery and What It Tells Us* is one such study.

Contemporary playwright John Mortimer uses imagery in *A Voyage Round My Father* when the Son turns to the audience to describe his father's garden: "Willow herb and thistles and bright poppies grew up. The fruit cage collapsed like a shaken temple and woods supported the tumbled netting. The rhododendrons and yew hedges grew high as a jungle, tall and dark and uncontrolled, lit with unexpected flowers."

imitation. The art of presenting behavior observed in others. Aristotle felt that human beings are naturally imitative, that they enjoy imitating and seeing imitation because they are curious to know what it is like to be someone or something else. Drama is one way of satisfying that curiosity. Imitation may involve playing a fictional character or a real person, as in Sophie Treadwell's *Machinal,* based on an actual murder case. It may even involve imitating another species, as in Paul Sills's *Story Theatre,* where actors became animals, birds, and insects as they acted out fables.

See MIMESIS.

immediacy. A sense of the action happening right now. This may be achieved by topical references, by a presentational playing style, by a sense of urgency in the tempo, or by a freshness in the entire look of the show.

See GUERRILLA THEATRE, LIVING NEWSPAPER, PRESENTATIONAL.

implicit directions. Stage directions implied in the lines of the play. In Pamela Hansford-Johnson's *Corinth House,* Madge, a former pupil of Miss Malleson, has come to plead with her old teacher to take her in and care for her. Although there is no stage direction in the script to tell Madge to clutch at Miss Malleson, the lines themselves are so beseeching that such a direction is implied. In fact, later, Miss Malleson asks Madge why she is touching her arm.

impressionism. The subjective creation of a scene or character by evoking sensory responses rather than by objectively recreating reality. The term was borrowed from a French school of painting that flourished from about 1870 to 1910. In literature, as in art, impressionism attempts to render the surface appearance of people and objects. In the theatre impressionism is used to create a mood with lighting and sound effects, the use of certain colors in the set and costumes, and evocative music. In Elizabeth Swados's *Runaways,* the chain-link fence and the graffiti-covered walls effectively give an impression of the emotional state of the characters. Although short-lived as a movement in the theatre, impressionism did give rise to expressionism.

Impressionistic criticism, which Anatole France called "the adventures of a sensitive soul among masterpieces," emphasized the critic's subjective response to a literary work. English writer E. M. Forster wrote much impressionistic criticism.

See CRITICISM, EXPRESSIONISM.

improvisation. A spontaneous scene or episode created by an actor or actors without a script. Improvisation may be used in response to something going wrong during a performance; it may be an exercise carried out at a director's or instructor's order; or it may be an actual performance by a troupe specializing in these techniques—for example, commedia dell'arte, The Compass Players, and The Second City. In rehearsal, it is a valuable tool for freeing up players, establishing bonds, and understanding difficult passages in a play. Don Eitner, directing James Goldman's *The Lion in Winter* at the Dallas Theatre Center in the 1970s, during rehearsal placed the actor playing Henry II at the top of a set of risers and the actors playing Henry's sons on the lower steps. As they improvised on the action of the play, the sons found themselves jockeying for position on the risers, attempting to reach Henry's riser and moving forward or backward as events in the play dictated their closeness to Henry's affections at a given moment. A favorite improvisation of many directors and instructors is the high/low status game devised by Keith Johnstone of London's Royal Court Theatre, in which a pair (or group) of actors, one playing high status and the other low, conduct a transaction wherein the status may shift or remain the same as the relationships are defined. This helps actors and students understand who dominates a scene and by what means.

See THEATRE GAMES.

incident light. Light falling on a surface—actor, furniture, or set—directly from above.

inciting incident, event. The first incident leading to the rising action of a play.

ingenue. The young, attractive, innocent female lead in a play, generally the romantic interest. Also, an actor who plays that type of part. In musicals it is often the dancing lead, such as Lois/Bianca in Samuel and Bella Spewack's *Kiss Me Kate.* The ingenue may be virginal or merely naive. Some ingenue roles are Muriel in Eugene O'Neill's *Ah, Wilderness!,* Kim in Michael Stewart's *Bye Bye Birdie,* and Dominica in Barbara Shotenfeld's *Catch Me If I Fall.*

See JUVENILE, LEADING LADY, SOUBRETTE.

inner stage. In Elizabethan times there may have been a stage behind the back wall, since many directions call for a discovery of someone there, revealed by drawing the curtain. But there is no evidence that it was more than a small alcove where the actor could wait to be discovered. The term is also applied to the Spanish theatre where such a recess might disclose a statue of the Virgin Mary or an empty tomb after the Resurrection.

intention. The objective an actor has in a scene. To achieve this objective, the actor must overcome an obstacle provided by the antagonist or by circumstances. Overcoming the obstacle supplies much of the action of a play. In Harold Pinter's *Old Times,* Kate has invited her former roommate Anna to dinner. Kate's intention is to renew their friendship, but an obstacle is set up when Anna teams with Kate's husband Deeley to annoy Kate and to provoke her into revealing her true feelings about Anna.

In rehearsal, a director may have an actor state the intention for each action. For example:

> A young girl left home alone enters her parents' bedroom: intention—to relieve her boredom.
> She opens a dresser drawer: intention—to satisfy her curiosity.
> She finds and reads an old letter: intention—to pry into her parents' lives.
> She takes the letter away with her: intention—to confront her parents later with the contents.

interlude. Originally, a play performed from the gallery of a manor house during a banquet in Elizabethan times. Most interludes were silly and diversionary. Later, in the Renaissance, the interlude was a short play given between the acts of a long play. In the late fifteenth century, playwright John Heywood formed a company called the Players of the King's Interludes, and they performed at festivals and in private houses. The arguments or subjects presented in these interludes were of five types: moral, or the struggle between vice and virtue for a human soul; political; pedagogical, as in John Redford's *The Marriage of Wit and Science;* historical, about the lives and deeds of English kings; and comic, as in Heywood's *The Play of the Weather.* Henry Medwall's *Fulgens and Lucres* was one of the most popular interludes.

See ARGUMENT.

interpretation. The discovery and determination of meaning in a literary work. In producing a play, the director determines which interpretation will be presented to the public. The director may consult a dramaturg or may ask the cast for their opinions, but usually the director has an interpretation in mind before beginning rehearsals. A director may interpret Bridget Boland's *The Prisoner* as the story of Cardinal Mindzenty's internment as a political prisoner or as an allegory for those who are imprisoned because they refuse to renounce their moral principles.

See ALLEGORY, DIRECTOR, DRAMATURG.

in the moment. Living the actions and words of a scene and not anticipating what comes next. An example of *not* being in the moment is the actor who, while talking to another, turns toward the phone, which is about to ring. An actor in the moment is listening so intently to the other actor that, when the phone does ring, it startles him or her.

See CONCENTRATION, FOCUS.

iris. A reducing mat used over the face of a spotlight in order to narrow the beam of light.

See SPOTLIGHT.

irony. Acknowledgment of the difference between reality and appearance. Dramatic irony means that the audience knows something relevant that the character does not. In Jay Presson Allen's adaptation of *The Prime of Miss Jean Brodie,* Jean is arguing with her young pupil Sandy over the school's art teacher, Teddy Lloyd. Jean considers Sandy unattractive and unloved when, in fact, the audience knows that Sandy has become Teddy's mistress, supplanting Jean.

See DRAMATIC IRONY.

J

jack. A wooden triangular brace hinged to the back of a flat to provide support. It is fastened to the floor by a stage screw and foot iron (hardware used in securing scenery).

See FLAT.

jackknife. A rolling cart used to change scenery, attached to the stage floor at one place and pivoted so that it can be moved on and off stage.

Jacobean revenge tragedy. A type of drama popular during the reign of James I of England (1603–1625) and said to reflect the permissiveness of the times, which placed an emphasis on the theatrical and the sensational rather than on the concept of humanity's tragic destiny. The main characters were sentimentalized and the plot was often wrenched to point a moral. In presenting the destructive power of evil, the plays focused on the baser aspects of human nature. There was frequent use of the play-within-the-play, or a paralleling of actions in two different places. The idea was to kill off nearly everyone by the play's end by as a great a variety of means as possible with one good character left to speak the moral. An outstanding example is a play still often staged, Thomas Middleton's *Women Beware Women.* At the Duke's banquet, Isabella is struck by a poisoned shower of gold, Guardino falls through a trapdoor, Livia is poisoned by incense, Fabritio is shot with an arrow, Hippolito falls on a sword, the Duke is poisoned accidentally, and Brancha commits suicide with a poisoned drink. Only the Cardinal is left to remind us that where lust reigns, a prince cannot.

See TRAGEDY.

jig. A song and dance routine, often with topical references, presented after the show in Elizabethan theatres.

See AFTERPIECE.

jog. A narrow flat or wing on a piece of scenery. It may be used to mask or fill in space between flats and a doorway. It is constructed in the same manner as a regular flat.

See FLIPPER.

juice. Jargon for electricity, as in the phrase "turn on the juice."

jumper. A cable connecting two or more lighting instruments or, temporarily, two circuits.

jump lines. When an actor speaks one or more lines ahead. This jump often confuses other members of the cast and at times omits crucial information or an entrance cue.

See CUE, EXPOSITION, IN THE MOMENT, SPEECHES.

juvenile. The male counterpart to the ingenue and her partner in the romantic plot. Also, an actor who plays such parts. Some juvenile roles are Richard in Eugene O'Neill's *Ah, Wilderness!,* Hugo in Michael Stewart's *Bye Bye Birdie,* and Wormy in Mary Chase's *Bernardine.* The juvenile is often the dancing lead, for example, Bill/Lucentio in Samuel and Bella Spewack's *Kiss Me Kate.*

See INGENUE, LEADING MAN, CONFIDANT.

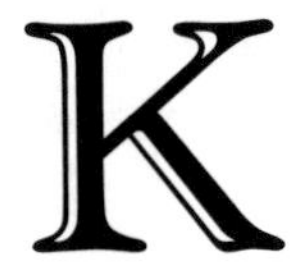

Kabuki. A popular form of theatre in Japan since the seventeenth century, it uses songs, dances, sketches, music, elaborate settings, and silk costumes. All the actors are men, and some specialize in playing women's parts. They must be skilled dancers and acrobats. Subjects of the plays range from epics of Japanese history, tragedies, and farces, to melodramas of the common people. The emphasis in Kabuki is on spectacle. Although Kabuki is an offshoot of Noh theatre, the actors are not masked but, instead, use very stylized makeup and wigs. The scene changes are effected by two stagehands, dressed in black, who are regarded by the audience as invisible.

The most popular Kabuki play remains Takeda Izumo's *Chusingura,* which has eleven acts and takes a full day to perform. It is based on a historical event in which forty-seven faithful followers avenged the wrongs done to their master.

See NOH.

katharsis. Alternate spelling of *catharsis,* the sense of release felt by the audience at the end of a tragedy.

See CATHARSIS.

key light. A light on an actor's face that appears to be coming from a source—lantern, lamp, fireplace—onstage, but which in fact is coming from conventional stage lighting instruments.

kitchen sink drama. A term used by critics to describe the realistic working-class plays of England's Arnold Wesker because so much of the action takes place in homely settings, such as the kitchen. One of Wesker's plays, *The Kitchen,* is actually set in the kitchen of a large restaurant. His work is earthy, protesting, energy-charged, political, and angry, showing a deep social concern. Wesker's most popular play is *Chips with Everything,* which uses the hierarchy of the armed services as a metaphor of the world.

See AGITPROP, ANGRY YOUNG MEN, DIDACTIC.

kleig light. A type of spotlight sold by the Kliegl brothers, but the term is used loosely for any bright stage light.

knife. The steel guide on a scenery cart that keeps it on the track.

kommos. A lament and response exchange between the chorus and the actors in Greek tragedy. In the first stasimon of Aeschylus' *Chorphoroe,* the principals kneel at the grave of Agamemnon and exchange recollections of his deeds, his murder, and the vengeance to come.

See STASIMON.

komos. An ancient drunken and ribald revelry in honor of Dionysus. The accompanying processions are said to be the origins of comedy in the theatre.

L

ladder. A hanging, ladderlike framework on which spotlights are mounted.

lamp. The proper name for a light bulb; also, the term for any lighting instrument, particularly a spotlight.

lash lines. Number-8 sash cords, used with staggered lash cleats (small metal hooks) to fasten one flat to another in the make-up of a unit of scenery.

See FLAT.

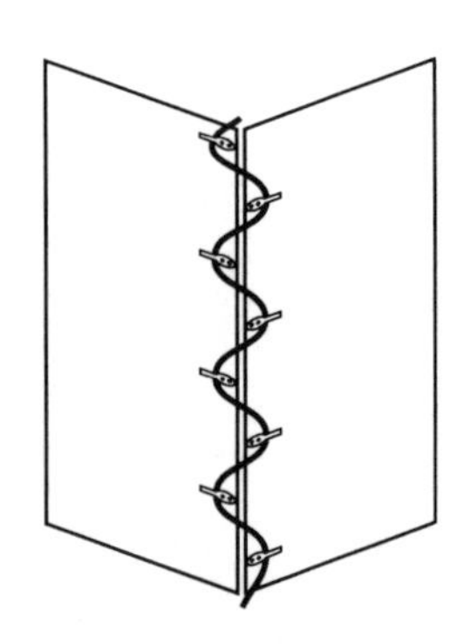

Lash lines, cleats, and flats

latecomers. Audience members who arrive after the play has started. Most theatres state in the program, on the ticket envelope, and on lobby signs that latecomers will not be seated until there is an appropriate pause in the performance. Such a policy ensures that those who have arrived on time will not be inconvenienced by the rudeness of those who have not.

lazzo. An Italian word, meaning "trick" or "joke." It refers to the bits of comic business and gimmicks performed by the clowns in the commedia dell'arte. Begun as improvisations, then, if popular with audiences, lazzi were incorporated into the repertoire of the performer. One such lazzo was to pretend to catch a fly on the wing and then eat it with lip-smacking gusto. Another was to turn a somersault while holding a glass of water and not spill a drop.

See ARLECCHINO, COMMEDIA DELL'ARTE, GIMMICK.

leading lady/man. The principal characters in a play, generally older than the ingenue and juvenile, but also attractive and part of the romantic plot. In musicals they are often the singers rather than the dancers, such as Fred/Petruchio and Lily/Kate in Samuel and Bella Spewack's *Kiss Me Kate.* Also the actors who play such parts.

See INGENUE, JUVENILE.

legitimate theatre. Straight drama, without songs, dances, or music. The term dates to the eighteenth-century English licensing laws, which covered only nonmusical shows. Hence, any show licensed was "legitimate." In modern times the term has come to mean stage shows as distinct from films and television.

leitmotiv. From the German, meaning "leading motive." In musical drama, especially that of Richard Wagner, a musical theme that recurs with the appearance of a character or situation. In nonmusical drama, a leitmotiv is the repetition of a word, a phrase, or an image. In Thornton Wilder's *The Long Christmas Dinner,* successive generations of the Bayard family repeat such phrases as "everything is encircled with ice," "I cried and cried," and "a glass of wine with you, sir." Wilder uses these leitmotivs to show the continuity of family life and to help unify the structure of his play.

Leko. A type of spotlight sold by Century-Strand. The term is applied generally to any ellipsoidal reflector spotlight. The Leko casts a sharply defined pool of light and is useful for lighting the stage from a distance.

See SPOTLIGHT.

libretto. From the Italian, meaning "little book." It refers to the dialog between the songs in a musical show. The writer is indicated in the credit after the words "book by." Moss Hart was responsible for the book for *Jubilee;* Guy Bolton and P. G. Wodehouse for *Oh, Kay!;* John O'Hara for *Pal Joey;* Thomas Meehan for *Annie;* Willy Russell for *Blood Brothers;* and James Lapine for *Into the Woods.*

lighting plot. Detailed plan by the lighting designer that includes a floor plan of the set with a longitudinal section—called an elevation—showing the height of the set, a lighting instrument schedule, and a control board cue sheet. The floor plan and longitudinal section show the location of each lighting instrument and the area lit. The longitudinal section also shows the vertical angles of the beams of light. The instrument schedule shows the type, wattage, outlet, dimmer, and color of each instrument. The cue sheet contains the dimmer readings for each instrument—a range from 100 percent for full up to 10 percent for very dim. The lighting technician uses the plot when running the lights for a show. Award-winning lighting designers include Tharon Musser, who was the first to bring computerized lighting boards to Broadway, and Jennifer Tipton.

light leak. An unwanted spill of light through a crack in the scenery or an open door on the set.

linear plot. One that follows a strict chronological order from start to finish with no flashbacks or flashforwards. Most plays are ordered in this manner. Dodie Smith's *Dear Octopus,* for example, opens on a Friday evening, continues on the next day, and concludes on Sunday of the same weekend.

See FLASHBACK.

line reading. The manner in which an actor delivers a line: the inflections, tone, volume, and pace used. Magaera, in G. B. Shaw's *Androcles and the Lion,* has been walking through the woods with her husband when suddenly she throws down her walking stick and says, "I won't go another step." The line may be said angrily, petulantly, wearily, pathetically, or matter of factly. The director may have the actor try it several ways before deciding on the reading to be used.

See CHOICES.

lines. The dialog for a play; the words the actors say in performance. In a rehearsal, once the cast is off book, members may call out the word "Line" if they need to be prompted.

See OFF BOOK.

little theatre. Amateur theatre, especially that developed by a community effort. Many catalogs of plays use this designation to indicate the level of ability required to perform particular plays. Early in the twentieth century, the little theatre movement in the United States was an attempt to use the European ideals of strong directing, noncommercial goals, and new staging techniques.

See COMMUNITY THEATRE.

liturgical theatre. Plays based on some aspect of the Roman Catholic liturgy. Beginning in European monasteries in the ninth century as short plays in Latin, these dramas continued for three hundred years with only the clergy, and occasionally choirboys, taking part. As settings they used the fixtures of the churches—nave, altar, choir loft, and stations of the cross.

See CORPUS CHRISTI PLAYS, CARNIVAL MASS, CYCLE PLAYS, MIRACLE PLAY, MYSTERY PLAY.

living newspaper. A topical revue of brief skits based on social and political issues of the day, devised in the 1930s in the United States by the WPA (Works Progress Administration) theatre project. The format spread to Great Britain where it was used for propaganda purposes during World War II.

See AGITPROP, DIDACTIC, REVUE.

load. The total power consumption in a circuit, measured in watts, or the total current requirements of a circuit, measured in amperes.

load in. To place the set on the stage where the play is to be performed. This includes dutching the seams and bolting the frames to the floor.

See DUTCHMAN, SET, STAGE CREW.

localize. To identify the place of the action in a play. This may be established by scenery or by dialog. In Lisette Lecat-Ross's *Dark Sun,* a play about racial misunderstanding in Soweto, the setting is an interior, but the playwright uses a background of recorded folk songs to create a sense of place.

long run. A show that continues to play for a long time because there is still a demand for tickets. In the early 1990s, Agatha Christie's *The Mouse Trap* had been running in London for forty years, and in New York City, the Tom Jones–Harvey Schmidt musical *The Fantasticks* had passed its thirtieth year. Other long-running shows include *Abie's Irish Rose, My Fair Lady,* and *A Chorus Line.*

low comedy. Although not a pejorative term, it does mean the opposite of high comedy; that is, it is physical rather than intellectual comedy. Some typical features are quarreling, drunkenness, infidelity, trickery, vulgarity, gossiping, and nagging.

The old comedy of Greece, with its connections to the ribaldry of the cult of Dionysus, serves as a good example of low comedy. For example, Aristophanes' *Ecclesiazusae* features an episode in which prostitutes, each one older and uglier than the one before, fight over a young man.

In Shakespeare's *The Merry Wives of Windsor,* the deception of Falstaff and the indignities he suffers are examples of low comedy. Modern examples include the sketches by Ralph G. Allen in *Sugar Babies* and S. J. Perelman's *The Beauty Part.*

lunchtime theatre. A type of performance given during the lunchtime of a workday. The trend started in London in the late 1960s when young actors and playwrights, looking for places to present their work, began using basements, upper stories, back rooms in pubs, and social clubs to stage short plays, usually of an experimental nature. One of the first of these lunchtime theatres was the Basement Theatre in Greek Street. The Cafe Theatre at the Bird and Bear Pub has put on such critically acclaimed works as Stephen Poliakoff's *Hitting Town.*

See AVANT-GARDE.

lyrics. The words of the songs in musical shows. The writers are called lyricists and important ones of the twentieth century include Otto Harbach, *Roberta, The Cat and the Fiddle* (music by Jerome Kern); Lorenz Hart, *Pal Joey, Simple Simon* (music by Richard Rodgers); Ira Gershwin, *Of Thee I Sing, Girl Crazy* (music by George Gershwin); Cole

Porter, *Anything Goes, Silk Stockings* (music by Cole Porter); Irving Berlin, *Call Me Madam, Annie Get Your Gun* (music by Irving Berlin); Alan Jay Lerner, *Brigadoon, My Fair Lady* (music by Frederick Loewe); and Stephen Sondheim, *Sweeney Todd, A Little Night Music* (music by Stephen Sondheim).

mainstage production. In a theatre complex having more than one performing space, the production mounted on the largest stage. In an academic situation, the major production of the school term, usually given more time and more money than, say, the workshop production of a student-written play.

See WORKSHOP PRODUCTION, ACADEMIC THEATRE.

make it larger. A direction to the actor to make the delivery of a line less subtle and more energetic.

See LINE READING.

make up. The verb *make up* means to put together a setting for a play.

See SCENERY.

makeup. The cosmetics that actors use onstage. Greasepaint, used as foundation or base for the rest of the makeup—lipstick, mascara, eyeliner, rouge, eye shadow, and powder—is easily blended but difficult to remove from skin and costume. Pancake, a compressed powder, is applied with a damp sponge and easily washed away. It cannot be blended, but it comes in a wide range of shades. Unlike greasepaint, pancake does not hold up well under very hot lights. Cream sticks are tubes of color that go on smoothly for highlights and shadows.

Applying straight makeup means using the cosmetics just to enhance, but not change, the natural features of the actor. Corrective makeup is used for a minor adjustment of facial features—for example, for shortening, lengthening, narrowing, or broadening the nose. Character makeup emphasizes character traits through created features, such as a stingy mouth, angry eyebrows, or sunken cheeks.

Makeup may also include the construction from latex (a liquid rubber used to form a flexible skin) of a different nose or ears, a bald pate, or a double chin. Beards or moustaches can be built up strand by strand from crepe (artificial) hair, and glued with spirit gum to the actor's face.

In a large company, technicians called makeup artists apply these cosmetics, but most actors know how to make up themselves, and many prefer to create and apply their own makeup. For Andrew Lloyd Webber's *Cats,* Paul Huntley and John Napier designed the elaborate makeup and wigs that turned dancers and singers into railroad cats and theatre cats and glamor cats and magical cats—cats of every color and description.

See GREASEPAINT.

manager. British term for the producer of a show. In Britain the term *producer* is used to indicate the director. Slowly the British are coming to use American terms, but in provincial repertory companies, the original terms are still used.

See DIRECTOR, PRODUCER.

mansions. Simple constructions on small platforms, representing such settings as Heaven, Hell, the House of a Disciple, or the Sea of Galilee. Used in medieval religious drama, they were positioned around the inside perimeter of churches. The actors, who were clergy, moved from mansion to mansion while the standing congregation turned to follow the action of each episode. When the plays moved out of the church building and into the town square, the mansions were set in a straight line along the square. They still depicted the settings, and the audience still stood in one place while the actors moved from mansion to mansion. The Coventry Cycle of forty-three plays evidently was staged on a permanent platform with the various mansions arranged along its length, but there is also evidence that the plays were taken on tour from town to town by strolling players. Records still exist of the costumes and props taken along.

See CORPUS CHRISTI PLAYS, CYCLE PLAYS, MEDIEVAL DRAMA, MIRACLE PLAY, MYSTERY PLAY.

mark. The mark, literally on the floor or established during rehearsal, from which actors deliver their lines.

See HIT YOUR MARK.

mask. **1.** A covering used to conceal all, or the upper part, of the face. In Greek tragedy, the mask was large and conveyed the age, sex, and emotional state of the character portrayed. Since an actor played more than one character, the mask was essential in maintaining the separate identity of each character.

In commedia dell'arte, the masks were highly stylized and usually covered just the upper part of the face, including the nose. The famed black Harlequin mask is often used as a design motif in the theatre or as a symbol of masquerade. The mask of Pantaloon has a grotesquely long nose, as befits the comic character.

In Japanese Noh theatre, the full mask is slightly smaller than the face, to reinforce its theatricalism.

Elaborate makeup is the extension of a mask. In Japanese Kabuki theatre, the makeup is highly stylized. For example, the actor portraying a delicate young lady would have his entire face tinted ivory white. Then, when "she" is transformed into a spider, she turns her back to the audience while a makeup man repaints her face. When she again looks to the audience, her face has become a mask of violent red spirals and black swirls.

See COMMEDIA DELL'ARTE, KABUKI, MAKEUP, NOH.

2. The flats or drapes used to block the sightlines of audience members so that they cannot see beyond the set of the play.

See SIGHTLINES.

masque. Growing out of the earlier mummers' plays, the Renaissance masque was at first rustic and depended on acrobatics, tumbling, miming, and antic capering about, blending pagan ritual and stories of folk heroes like Robin Hood or St. George. Even the nobility took part, dressing up and masking. By the reign of Henry VIII, however, the Italian style of masque, with its elaborate staging and ornamented speech, had replaced the earlier form. The principal writer of the masque in England was Ben Jonson (early seventeenth century), whose stage designer was the famous architect Inigo Jones. Jonson's first effort, *The Masque of Blackamoors,* appealed to both the eye and ear with its succession of rapidly changing scenes, tableaux crowded with beautifully costumed and wigged figures, delightful music, dances, pantomime, acrobatics, clowns, music, and a mix of professional actors and talented gentry. It cost the then exorbitant sum of three thousand pounds. Martha Clarke's recent *The Garden of Earthly Delights* owes much to the Renaissance masque tradition.

See MUMMER.

mat. Shutter or matting material that is used on the face of a spotlight lens to change the size or shape of the beam cast onto the set.

See GOBO, SPOTLIGHT.

matinee. A theatrical performance given in the afternoon. Most theatres offer a matinee on Saturday afternoon and another on a weekday. Sometimes, during a long run, the understudy, rather than the star, will take the afternoon performances.

See UNDERSTUDY.

medieval drama. Classical drama virtually ceased to exist after the fall of Rome, but drama was reborn during the medieval period, and once again out of a religious ceremony. Some dialog was inserted into the Easter Mass to hold the attention of the congregation not well versed in Latin. The device proved popular and was then used in other Masses. Eventually, stories from the Bible were dramatized, and as these became more elaborate and distracted from the Mass, they were moved outside the church building onto the steps, and then into the village square, and even taken to nearby towns.

See CORPUS CHRISTI PLAYS, CYCLE PLAYS, INTERLUDE, MANSIONS, MIRACLE PLAY, MORALITY PLAY, MYSTERY PLAY.

meet cute, to. The situation in a romantic comedy in which the principals first encounter one another with clever stage business, witty dialog, or both. In Arthur Laurents's *Invitation to a March,* soon-to-be-married Norma has fallen asleep on the beach in front of her family's summer cottage. The handyman Aaron passes by, sees her, and steals a kiss. She awakens to ask, "Are you a prince?" The device of meeting cute serves to make the principals engaging to an audience.

See BUSINESS, INGENUE, JUVENILE.

mekane. The machine, in classical Greek theatre, for lowering actors into the playing area. It was a kind of crane suspended from the top of the skene building.

See DEUS EX MACHINA, SKENE.

melodrama. Drama originating in nineteenth-century England that relies heavily on sensationalism and sentimentality. Melodrama may follow the structure of tragedy, but tends to feature action more than motivation, stock characters, and a strict black-and-white view of morality—that is, virtue is rewarded and evil punished. The typical pattern of such plays involves provocation: an incident, often caused by the jealousy or greed of the villain, that sets the plot in motion (for example, a banker who holds the mortgage on the heroine's home will throw her out if she does not yield to his lustful demands); pangs: the suffering of the good and innocent characters (a clerk is accused of stealing when actually the banker, who is jealous of the clerk, has taken the money himself); and penalty: a last-minute reversal of the situation (the clerk is cleared of the charges and rushes to the rescue of the homeless heroine). Since melodrama is often participatory theatre, the audience is encouraged to hiss the villain and cheer the hero.

A perennially popular melodrama has been *The Drunkard,* credited to "P. T. Barnum and Others." Recently, Rupert Holmes's *The Mystery of Edwin Drood* and Stephen Sondheim's *Sweeney Todd* have been presented as melodramas. The adjective *melodramatic* is applied to those elements in plays that are farfetched, bathetic rather than pathetic, and presented with an exaggerated acting style.

See DECLAIM, PARTICIPATORY THEATRE, PATHOS, TRAGEDY, VILLAIN.

Melpomene. The muse of tragedy, one of the nine muses of Mount Parnassus, believed by the Greeks to inspire those working in the arts or sciences.

See THALIA.

method acting. An introspective approach to acting based on the system developed by Constantin Stanislavsky for the Moscow Art Theatre early in the twentieth century. The Method, as it is called, came to prominence in America in the 1930s after its adoption by the Actors' Studio in New York City. There is much controversy about the Method. Some critics see it as a much-needed reaction against artificial acting styles popular at the time of its inception. Others protest that it makes the actor too self-involved and is suitable only for the kind of play Stanislavsky directed. A parody of the Method has an actor constantly asking the director, "But what's my motivation?" for even the simplest action in a play. Stanislavsky said that the difference between the "external" acting of his time (all on the surface, with no inner feeling for the truth of the part) and his own method is the difference between seeming and being.

See AFFECTIVE MEMORY, ACTORS' STUDIO, EMOTIONAL RECALL, MOTIVATION, OBJECTIVE.

middle comedy. A transitional form of Greek drama (400–338 B.C.) between old comedy and new comedy. Characteristics include ignoring the cult of Dionysus, reducing political and topical references, emphasizing the pleasures of the bed and the table, and using more everyday speech. There was less use of *parabasis* (the coming forward of the chorus to comment) and, instead, the chorus was used in musical interludes. Over forty authors and six hundred plays of middle comedy are known, but the only two surviving plays are Aristophanes' *Ecclesiazusae* and *Plautus.* These, however, do show that middle comedy had more plot development than the old comedy it replaced.

See CHORUS, CLASSICAL DRAMA, COMEDY, NEW COMEDY, OLD COMEDY, PARABASIS, SATIRE.

mime. From the Greek word *mimos,* meaning "representation." It is generally taken to mean acting without words, but in ancient Rome it meant a comic show with strong emphasis on action and gesture. In modern times mime is derived from commedia dell'arte, where the buffoonery, slapstick, and coarse humor made for a rowdy entertainment very unlike the disciplined, stylized movements of later mimes like Marcel Marceau and Jean-Louis Barrault. Most large cities have street mimes, performing in white makeup, imitating passersby or presenting the cliché of the person trapped in a box that keeps getting smaller. Samuel Beckett's *Act Without Words I: A Mime for One Player* contains only stage directions; no words are provided for the actor.

See BUSINESS, COMMEDIA DELL'ARTE, FABULA ATTELLANA, PANTOMIME.

mimesis. The Greek word meaning *imitation,* the term is used in criticism when discussing Aristotle's theory of imitation, or the creative process—that is, not merely copying behavior but representing the truth about life.

See IMITATION.

minimal setting. A stage setting that uses methods other than the box set. One method is the cyclorama or arras background of hung fabric. Other methods include an abstract set, which merely suggests the locality; a painted backdrop; and detail scenery. The minimal setting may be used for economical reasons, or because the play being done lends itself best to such a setting.

See ABSTRACT SET, ARRAS SETTING, BACKDROP, BOX SET, CYCLORAMA, DETAIL SCENERY.

miracle play. A type of medieval drama that depicted some miraculous event from the life of a saint. The only surviving play, one from the English Digby Cycle, is based on the life of Saint Mary Magdalene. There is known to have been a play called *Santa Katarina* performed about A.D. 1100 in Dunstable, England.

See CORPUS CHRISTI PLAYS, CYCLE PLAYS, MEDIEVAL DRAMA, MORALITY PLAY, MYSTERY PLAY.

mise-en-scène. From the French, meaning the "action of putting on the stage." It refers to the total environment of a play—the sets, costumes, blocking, visual effects, and props, and the composition of these elements. The term also refers to the "look" of a play at any given moment in a performance. A famous example of mise-en-scène is the 1977 New York City production of Anton Chekhov's *The Cherry Orchard* devised by director Andrei Serban and designers Santo Loquasto and Jennifer Tipton. Instead of a box set, a white cyclorama provided the background, an arctic-white carpet covered the stage floor, and the actors and furniture were arranged in groups, like pieces of sculpture, around the stage.

See CYCLORAMA.

mixed-media performance. A presentation that mixes live performers with electronic elements, such as projected slides, filmstrips, films, videotapes, and recorded music. The London production of the Tim Rice–Benny Andersson–Bjorn Ulvaeus musical *Chess* used animations of a chess match projected on large-screen monitors to comment on the action of the play. The form is also called multimedia.

See HAPPENING.

Momus. The Greek god of ridicule, and the inspiration of clowns. The term became a generic name for *clown,* and eventually was used by a commedia character.

See CLOWN CHARACTER.

monolog. A work written to be spoken by just one person. This may be full length, as in a one-man or one-woman show, or it may simply be a solo passage within a longer work. In Samuel Beckett's *Krapp's Last Tape,* there is just one character; in Robert Patrick's *Kennedy's Children,* five characters spend an afternoon in a bar, each speaking in monolog and at no time interacting with each other.

See SOLILOQUY.

morality play. A dramatized allegory developed in fifteenth-century England, in which the vices and virtues are personified as they battle for a human soul. The best-known example is *Everyman,* but others are *All for Money* and *Morality of Welth and Helth.* Christopher Marlowe's *Dr. Faustus,* performed in 1588, borrows from earlier morality plays.

See MEDIEVAL DRAMA.

motif. A recurrent character, incident, or concept in literature: the rags-to-riches motif; the girl disguised as a boy, used so often by Shakespeare; or the twins separated at, or shortly after, birth, used for comedy by Shakespeare in *The Comedy of Errors,* and by Willy Russell for tragedy in *Blood Brothers.* The term *leitmotiv* generally refers to an incident that recurs within a single work.

See LEITMOTIV.

motivation. The reason a character does something. Audiences expect sufficient reasons, plausible for the character's personality and experiences, for each important action. If a character does things that seem inappropriate, the character is said to be unmotivated. In Sophocles' *Electra,* Electra is motivated by a desire to see her father's murder avenged. In Shakespeare's *Macbeth,* people are murdered because Lady Macbeth wants desperately for her husband to be king. In Vera Caspary's *Laura,* adapted with George Sklar from her novel, police detective Mark McPherson is motivated to solve the mystery of Laura's death not merely because it's his job but also because he has fallen in love with her portrait.

See METHOD ACTING, PLOT.

motley. A suit of more than one color worn by clowns in the commedia. The costumes of Harlequin at first were varicolored patches, darker than the background fabric, and sewn here and there on the jacket and breeches. By the seventeenth century, the patches had become blue, red, and green triangles arranged in a symmetrical pattern. The term also refers to the multicolored suit of a court jester. In Shakespeare's *As You Like It,* the melancholy lord Jaques meets Touchstone, a fool, in the woods and proclaims, "Oh that I were a fool./I am ambitious for a motley coat."

See COMMEDIA DELL'ARTE, CLOWN CHARACTER, FOOL, HARLEQUIN.

movement. Stage blocking, or the movements of the actors onstage as the play progresses. Movement conveys meaning—agitated pacing, eager running, reluctant foot-dragging—and provides visual variety. The term also refers to the action of the play as it advances from event to event.

See BLOCKING, BUSINESS, DIRECTOR, PLOT.

muff. To say a line wrong, either by mixing up the words or mispronouncing them.

See FLUFFED LINE, GOES UP.

mugging. Using exaggerated facial expressions as directed for comic effect, out of a desire to upstage another actor, or because of bad acting technique.

See HAM, HISTRIONICS, UPSTAGING.

multiple settings. More than one setting on a stage at the same time. In medieval drama, this might be a series of mansions on a platform. In France, the convention of *décor simultané* afforded the director a variety of entrances, each signifying to the audience a different locale. In this century, English playwright Alan Ayckbourn has used a multilevel setting for several of his plays. In *How the Other Half Loves,* two couples have their living rooms on the stage at the same time. The couples pass without seeing each other. At one point two dinner parties, on different nights but involving the same guests, are enacted simultaneously with the table at center stage being in each couple's dining room. The timing by the actors must be impeccable to make it work, but it provides delightful farce, due in no small part to the ingenuity of the multiple settings.

See FARCE, SET.

mummer. An actor who participates in a mumming play—that is, a play depicting the death and resurrection of a folk hero—often St. George.

Although the form probably originated in early pagan springtime ritual, the earliest record of it is in the eighteenth century. One hundred years later villages across England performed such plays. The actors wore blackface and only men took part. Roles were often passed down from father to son. Usually included in the entertainment was the morris dance, a vigorous dance performed by men in costumes ornamented with ribbons and bells. Standard characters in the dance were the fool, the hobbyhorse (it was believed that any woman who touched the horse would be favored in childbirth), and the betty. Sometimes the performers sold "lord of misrule" badges to the crowds and used the money for drink.

See CONVENTION, MASQUE.

music. One of the six qualitative elements of drama, according to Aristotle. By *music* he meant the rhythm of speeches and the rhythm and melody of the choral odes that served to embellish tragedy.

See QUALITATIVE ELEMENTS OF DRAMA.

musical theatre. A type of entertainment fusing elements of ballad opera, early burlesque, and minstrel shows. Many of the plays might be called musical comedies—for example, Richard Rodgers and Oscar Hammerstein's *Oklahoma!,* Abe Burrows's *Guys and Dolls,* Irving Berlin's *Annie Get Your Gun,* and George Abbott's *The Pajama Game.* Others, especially of the past few years, are decidedly not comic. These include Tom Eyen and Henry Krieger's *Dreamgirls,* Alain Boublil and Claude-Michel Schönberg's *Les Misérables,* and Stephen Sondheim's *Follies.* Most musical plays have a plot, called the book, that is carried forward by some dialog and songs that arise out of the dialog. Andrew Lloyd Webber, however, has written a number of successful shows (for example, *Evita* and *Song and Dance*) that he calls "through-sung," that is, there is no dialog and only the songs carry the plot forward. From the 1920s to the present, the musical play has proved one of the most popular forms of stage entertainment.

See BALLAD OPERA, BURLESQUE, INGENUE, JUVENILE, LIBRETTO, LYRICS, SOUBRETTE.

music hall. Popular entertainment featuring a succession of acts, the music hall began in London in the "song and supper rooms" of Queen Victoria's reign. Women were admitted only if they gave name and address, and then they had to sit in a screened gallery. The performers were men who sang ballads, madrigals, and popular selections from operas, accompanied by piano and harmonium. Next came the variety saloon, licensed by the magistrates and offering a mixture of opera, drama, and farce with music and dancing to finish up. Then came the tavern concert rooms, which provided vocalists, impersonators, comic singers, minstrels, ventriloquists, acrobats, magicians, and dancers. The music hall developed from this background, and it offered the working classes, women included, entertainment and refreshments. Liquor sales paid for the entertainment. A chairman presided, announcing the acts and keeping order among the impatient crowd. The first turn might be the burlesque of some opera, followed by a singer of comic songs, and then a ballet featuring commedia characters. By the 1860s, there were twenty-eight music halls in London and three hundred more throughout England. Women performers now participated and, in the fashionable areas of the city, lavish music halls were built that could seat more than a thousand. Famous performers at the turn of the century were Marie Lloyd, Harry Lauder, and Harry Champion. The licensing laws of 1902 barring drinking, and the advent of motion pictures brought about the end of the music hall, although the Palladium in London still offers the old-fashioned variety show.

See COMMEDIA DELL'ARTE, VAUDEVILLE.

mystery play. A play concerned with biblical themes, especially events connected with the birth, life, death, and resurrection of Christ. Sometimes confused with the miracle play, since both have religious subjects. When mystery plays were moved from the church building into the town square, they developed into the cycle plays that told a story from creation to the last judgment.

See CHURCH DRAMA, CORPUS CHRISTI PLAYS, CYCLE PLAYS, LITURGICAL THEATRE, MEDIEVAL DRAMA, MIRACLE PLAY.

myth. A system of belief that accounts for the creation of the world and the operation of the universe. Also, a traditional tale involving legendary figures and archetypes. Aristotle used the word *myth* to describe the plot of a tragedy. Plays like Aeschylus's *The Seven Against Thebes,* Sophocles' *Philoctetes,* and Euripides' *Mad Heracles* depend on Greek myth for inspiration and understanding. Medieval drama was drawn from Christian myth, and many modern playwrights use classical and Christian myth and legend to support the material of their plays. In

Jean Giraudoux's *Ondine,* the principal character is the spirit of the sea embodied in a lovely young girl. G. B. Shaw's *Pygmalion* alludes to the Greek myth of the sculptor who fell in love with his own creation. Eugene O'Neill's *Mourning Becomes Electra* reworks the Electra myth. T. S. Eliot's *The Elder Statesman* echoes *Oedipus at Colonus,* and the Frederick Loewe–Alan Jay Lerner musical *Camelot* makes use of the legends of King Arthur.

See ARCHETYPAL CHARACTER.

narrator. A character outside the action of a play who explains or comments on events. In effect, such a person is the modern equivalent of the chorus in Greek drama. The most famous example is the Stage Manager in Thornton Wilder's *Our Town,* who comments on events of the play. Other plays that use this device are Peter Nichols's *A Day in the Death of Joe Egg* and *Forget-Me-Not Lane,* Stephen Sondheim's *Into the Woods,* and Robert Bolt's *A Man for All Seasons.*

See CHORUS, PRESENTATIONAL.

nativity play. A play in the cycle of mystery plays, dealing with events surrounding the birth of Christ. *The Second Shepherds Play,* a story of shepherds tending their flocks on the hills around Bethlehem and being called by angels to see the Christ Child, is a nativity play.

See CYCLE PLAYS, MYSTERY PLAY.

naturalism. A form of realism that dispenses with theatrical conventions in order to present a "slice of life." The playwright attempts to present life with complete detachment. There is great attention to detail in stage design. Underlying naturalistic drama is the notion that environment determines human fate. Naturalism began in the theatre in the late nineteenth century with such plays as Henri Becque's *Les Corbeaux,* Maxim Gorki's *The Lower Depths,* and August Strindberg's *Miss*

Julie. By the early twentieth century, the movement had been absorbed into realism.

See EXPRESSIONISM, REALISM.

nautical drama. A kind of romantic melodrama popular in England in the late eighteenth and early nineteenth centuries. It involved the usual characters of melodrama: innocent victim, ruthless villain, and stalwart hero. In nautical drama, the hero was a sailor, usually away at sea, maybe even presumed dead, who arrives home in the nick of time to save the damsel in distress. The form was burlesqued in Charles Dickens's *Nicholas Nickleby* when Nicholas joins a theatrical troupe performing such dramas. Tobias Smollett's *The Reprisal of the Tars of Old England* and Douglas Jerrold's *Black Eyed Susan* are examples of the form.

See MELODRAMA, VILLAIN.

neoclassicism. Drama imitative of Greek and Roman classical models. It was popular in France in the seventeenth and eighteenth centuries and followed these principles: verisimilitude, or the appearance of truth; purity of dramatic types, with no mingling of forms; the five-act play structure; decorum; didacticism, or drama for the purpose of teaching moral lessons; and strict adherence to the unities of time, place, and action. Outstanding practitioners were Pierre Corneille *(The Illusion),* Jean Racine *(Andromaque),* and, in England, Oliver Goldsmith *(She Stoops to Conquer).*

See CLASSICAL DRAMA, UNITIES.

new comedy. The principal dramatic form in Greece from about 330 B.C. to 150 B.C. It evolved from middle comedy and was a comedy of manners, depicting the private lives of the leisure class. The plot usually involved young lovers, those who would thwart them, and a happy ending. Stock characters included the loyal slave, the deceitful slave, the boor, the foundling, twins, the miser, the bold adventurer, and the venal courtesan. The structure had a prologue followed by five acts and a chorus used only to entertain between the acts. Historians believe a raised stage was used, and the orkestra area no longer held the altar of Dionysus. In fact, new comedy had no connection with the cult of Dionysus. In the staging there were no interior scenes, and all action took place before an exterior representing two houses separated by an *angiportum.* The leading writers of new comedy were Philemon of Syracuse *(The Ghost, Merchant),* Diphilus of Sinope *(Lot Drawers, Heracles),* Apollodorus of Carystus *(The Claimant, Mother-in-Law),* and the most famous of them, Menander, whose *The Grouch* was found complete in this century. Fragments of three of his other plays exist and nine survive in the imitations of the Roman playwrights Plautus and Terence.

See ANGIPORTUM, FARCE, MIDDLE COMEDY, OLD COMEDY, STOCK CHARACTERS.

Noh (No) theatre. Literally, "highly skilled or accomplished." The most important form of Japanese drama. The Noh play began as a religious ceremony in the fourteenth century. Over the next three hundred years, 240 plays were written that make up the standard repertory. There are five types of Noh and generally one of each type is presented at a religious festival: a play of praise to a god; a play about a warrior hero; a play about a woman, with a male actor in women's clothes; a play of ghosts; and a play with warlike dancing that ends peacefully in thanksgiving for the occasion of the festival.

The plays are highly stylized, depending on music, lavish costumes, mime, and masks. The stage is raised and has four pillars supporting a roof. To one side a small balcony holds a chorus of ten singers, and at the back a smaller stage holds the musicians and stagehands. There is no scenery and the actors enter and exit along a kind of bridge that leads from the dressing rooms. Noh provides a full day's entertainment as the five plays and the short, farcical interludes, called *kyogen,* take seven hours to perform.

See DRAG, KABUKI, MASK, MIME.

noises off. Any sound effects needed for a dramatic production, from the thunder sheet to tape-recorded rainfall. Also, stage direction to indicate voices, usually indistinguishable, of offstage characters, especially a crowd. Contemporary playwright Michael Frayn titled a farce *Noises Off* because so much of the action takes place on a set representing the backstage of a play in rehearsal and then in performance.

See EFFECTS, THUNDER SHEET.

objective. The goal a character has in a particular scene or throughout a play. In Shakespeare's *Othello,* Iago, mad with jealousy at being passed over for promotion, intends to punish Othello, no matter what harm he may cause in achieving that objective. Sometimes also called "intention," although an actor's intention in a scene may differ from his or her goal. An actor may, for instance, try to gain a particular response from the audience while the objective of the character may be to confront another character.

See INTENTION, OBSTACLE.

obligatory scene. A scene the playwright has led the audience to expect, one that answers questions raised earlier in the play. There is a saying in the theatre that if a gun is hanging on the wall in the first scene, it had better be fired by the last scene. The obligatory scene is sometimes called the *scène-à-faire,* or "the scene to do." In murder mysteries the audience expects a scene in which the murderer is named and the methods and motive are revealed. In Lillian Hellman's *The Children's Hour,* Karen and Martha operate a girls' boarding school and are accused by a vindictive student of having an "unnatural affection" for each other. Audience members know that Mary, the accuser, is angry at being punished for lying, but they cannot help wondering about the relationship between Karen and Martha. The two women lose their libel suit against Mary's aunt, who has spread rumors against them. Even though audience members know the testimony has been perjured, they still wonder about the two women. In the obligatory scene, Martha acknowledges to Karen that she has loved her as more than a friend.

See DENOUEMENT.

obstacle. A character or situation in a play that creates conflict, that delays or prevents another character from achieving an objective. In T. S. Eliot's *The Cocktail Party,* Lavinia, the aggrieved wife, wishes to be seen as blameless, betrayed, fragile, in need of solace and coddling. The obstacle to her objective is no-nonsense psychiatrist Harcourt-Reilly, who insists on confronting her with the truth of her relationship with her husband.

See INTENTION, OBJECTIVE.

off/on book. When an actor has the lines of his or her part completely memorized, the actor is off book; when an actor still needs the script, the actor is on book. To "sit on book" is to prompt the actors in rehearsal.

off/on stage. When off, an actor is out of sight of the audience; when on, an actor is in sight of the audience.

Off Broadway. Commercial theatre productions away from the central theatre district in New York City. The term came into use in the 1950s and refers both to the plays and to the theatres. The plays are often experimental or in need of a more intimate setting than the large spaces of Broadway theatres. Sometimes, a play does so well Off Broadway that it moves to a bigger house. Some Off Broadway theatres are the John Houseman Theatre, Sullivan Street Theatre, and the Circle in the Square. Award-winning and long-running plays that premiered Off Broadway are Bertolt Brecht and Kurt Weill's *The Threepenny Opera,* Alfred Uhry's *Driving Miss Daisy,* Terrence McNally's *Frankie and Johnnie in the Clair de Lune,* and Robert Harling's *Steel Magnolias.*

Because many playwrights and producers feel that Off Broadway is becoming too expensive and conventional, Off-Off Broadway has developed, using warehouses, church basements, lofts, and all manner of found space for small productions, usually in short runs.

See AVANT-GARDE, BROADWAY, FOUND SPACE.

old comedy. Comedy that had its origins in the choruses and processions of the cult of Dionysus and was performed publicly in Athens by 487 B.C. The loosely constructed plots satirized the issues of the time. There was much buffoonery and coarseness as well as elements of fantasy—for example, the chorus dressed as animals. Each play had a prolog in which the "happy idea" was announced. Then came the *parados,* or entrance of the chorus. Next came the *agon* in which the happy idea was debated and a decision reached. This was followed by the *parabasis* in which the chorus came forward and addressed the audience, expressing the playwright's view of things. Next came episodes in which the happy idea was put into practice. Finally, there was the romantic union and celebration.

Although there are records of playwrights Magnes of Athens *(Gall-Flies, Harp-Players),* Cratius of Athens *(Caught in a Storm, Chirons),* and others, the greatest is considered to be Aristophanes, who wrote forty plays, eleven of which have survived. The most often performed is *Lysistrata,* but others are *Clouds, Wasps, Birds,* and *Frogs.*

See AGON, CHORUS, GAMOS, KOMOS, MIDDLE COMEDY, NEW COMEDY, PARABASIS.

oleo. The backdrop used in vaudeville performances. Also, the front drop painted with advertisements.

See BACKDROP, DROP, VAUDEVILLE.

olio. Literally, a miscellaneous collection, usually of musical selections. Often, during the intermission of a melodrama, the company performed a series of short musical numbers, mostly comical, and then asked the audience to join in singing such songs as "Daddy Wouldn't Buy Me a Bow Wow."

See MELODRAMA.

olivette. A box floodlight that can be mounted on a stand or hung by a chain from a pipe batten. Largely replaced by newer, more efficient floodlights, it can still be found in many older theatres.

See BATTEN, FLOODLIGHT.

Olivier Awards. The British equivalent of the Tony Awards for theatre. The awards are named for the late Sir Laurence Olivier, English actor, director, and producer. He was knighted in 1947 and made a baron in 1970, the first actor to receive this honor.

See TONY AWARDS.

one-act play. A short play, running from fifteen minutes to one hour, that is performed without an intermission or a change of scenery. It may be a curtain raiser to another, longer play, as is John M. Synge's *Riders to the Sea,* or it may play in tandem with a play of equal length, just as Murray Schisgal's *The Typists* and *The Tiger* often do.

one-man, one-woman show. A performance by a single actor—though there may be live or recorded musical accompaniment. The show may be a collage, such as Brian Bedford's *The Lunatic, The Lover and the Poet,* consisting of excerpts from Shakespeare's poems and plays. It may be autobiographical, such as Spalding Gray's *Swimming to Cambodia.* It may be musical, such as Phyllis Newman's *The Mad Woman of Central Park West,* written with Arthur Laurents. Or it may be an impersonation, such as Julie Harris playing Emily Dickinson in William Luce's *The Belle of Amherst.* The term generally is not applied to one-character plays, such as Willy Russell's *Shirley Valentine.*

See MONOLOG, PERFORMANCE ART.

openers. The characters who are onstage at, or shortly after, the beginning of the play.

See BEGINNERS.

opening. The first public performance of a play. There may have been workshop versions of it or previews before the official opening.

See GOES UP.

operetta. A type of theatre, developed from the French *opéra bouffe,* with music, songs, and, often, dance. Unlike opera, operetta contains spoken dialog, is lighthearted or comic, and usually ends happily. An early example is Richard Sheridan's *The Duenna* (1775). The most popular have been the romantic operettas of Victor Herbert *(Naughty Marietta),* Sigmund Romberg *(The Student Prince),* Rudolph Friml *(Rose Marie),* and Johann Strauss, Jr. *(Die Fledermaus),* and the satirical works of W. S. Gilbert and Arthur Sullivan *(The Mikado).* Although the form was most popular in the late nineteenth and early twentieth centuries, operettas are still frequently performed. Rich Besoyan has gently spoofed the form in his *Little Mary Sunshine* and *The Student Gypsy.*

See COMIC OPERA.

orkestra, orchestra. Originally, a circular place on the floor of the classical Greek stage where the chorus danced. The altar of Dionysus was located in the center, in front of the *proskenion.* By the era of new comedy, the altar had been eliminated and the orkestra was no longer used.

In the classical Roman theatre, the orkestra was reduced to a semicircle roughly located where today's stage apron is, and it was not used.

Now the orchestra is the ground floor seating in an auditorium.

overture. The music played before a musical play begins; generally it is a medley of tunes from the show to be performed.

P

pace. The speed with which a play is performed. Comedies generally are played faster than serious plays. The latter require time for the audience to absorb crucial information. The pace of any play can be quickened by a faster picking up of cues.

See CUES.

pageant wagon. A four- or six-wheeled, horse-drawn wagon used to move the settings of the medieval cycle plays to the next stopping place within the town. The wagon held a two-story scaffold. The lower part was curtained off and used as a changing place for the actors; the upper, reached by an outside ladder or inside trapdoor, was set with the particular mansion(s) for each play. The banner of the sponsoring guild was carried in front of the wagon. Eventually the word *pageant* came to mean any elaborate street procession or a series of tableaux across a stage.

See CYCLE PLAYS, GUILDS, MANSIONS, TABLEAU.

Pantaloon. Also Pantalone. A comic character in the commedia, traditionally garbed in red tights, a loose black cape, red wool bonnet or skullcap, and Turkish slippers. He wears a beard and a mask with a long, crooked nose. The character is a man of business, married to a young, pretty woman who deceives him. Sometimes, he has a young daughter who causes him much worry, and pert servant girls often steal his silver and invite their lovers into the house in secret. In the Harlequinade he was always the butt of the clown's jokes.

See COMMEDIA DELL'ARTE, HARLEQUINADE.

pantomime. From *Pantomimus,* a type of solo performer in ancient Rome who used movement and gesture to convey a series of characters in a retelling of a Greek legend. Eighteenth-century pantomime included dancing and silent mimicry with musical accompaniment and elaborate scenery and special effects. Serious scenes alternated with comic ones featuring Harlequin doing magic tricks with a wand or secret spell.

A traditional Christmas entertainment in England, pantomime derives from the commedia. Often called simply panto, it is an extravaganza based on a fairy tale, such as Cinderella or Aladdin, and interpolating popular songs, topical references, ballet, and acrobatics. It requires the role of Principal Boy to be played by a young, pretty girl and the Dame to be played by a man, often a famous comedian like Stanley Baxter, Patrick Cargill, or Bernard Crimmins.

See COMMEDIA DELL'ARTE, DRAG, HARLEQUINADE, MIME, PANTS PART, PRINCIPAL BOY.

pants part. A male role played by a female. In England called "breeches part." In Johann Strauss, Jr.'s *Die Fledermaus,* Prince Orlof is usually played by a woman, and the Principal Boy in pantomime is always played by a young, pretty girl, often a rising ingenue. Pants parts include the temporary disguises of Shakespeare's Viola and Rosalind, and the Hamlets of Sarah Bernhardt and Dame Judith Anderson.

See DRAG.

papering the house. Giving out free tickets to fill the house for a performance.

See ANNIE OAKLEY, CLAQUE, COMP, DRESSING THE HOUSE.

par. Short for parabolic reflector lamp. It is made of molded heat-resistant glass that can be used safely outdoors, even where cold rain strikes the hot surface of the lamp. Indoors, its built-in reflector makes it an economical choice for small to medium-sized theatres, and colored bulbs eliminate the need for gels. While pars work well in strip lighting or as floodlights, they are not suitable as spotlights because of the difficulty in controlling the beam.

See GEL, BORDER LIGHTS, SPOTLIGHT.

parabasis. In old Greek comedy, it was the coming forward of the chorus to address the audience, voicing the thoughts of the playwright on various matters of interest. By middle comedy, the practice was seldom used and new comedy dropped the device completely. In Aristophanes' *Clouds,* the playwright uses the *parabasis* to have the chorus explain that *Clouds* is his best play, to express his views on comedy writing and his pride in his art, and to call on the audience to worship the clouds of the air for their service to Athens.

See CHORUS, MIDDLE COMEDY, NEW COMEDY, OLD COMEDY.

parade. The brief sketch performed by fairgrounds actors outside their booth or tent to entice spectators to pay and see the show.

See BARKER.

parados. In Greek tragedy, the entering song or dance of the chorus. By new comedy the *parados* had disappeared because the chorus no longer had a formal entry but served mainly to entertain the audience between acts.

In the *parados* of Aeschylus's *The Suppliant Women,* the chorus of fifty Danaids enters a sacred grove near Argos and prays to Zeus for help in escaping the lustful, violent sons of Aegyptus who pursue them.

See CHORUS, CLASSICAL DRAMA.

paraskena, parascenia. In the classical Greek theatre, the wings or flanking pieces of the skene building.

See SKENE.

parody. The mockery of a writing style by an exaggerated imitation of its predominant characteristics. *The New Yorker's* theatre critic Edith Oliver describes Arthur Kopit's *Road to Nirvana* as inspired ridicule and parody. The style being parodied is that of David Mamet, especially that used in *Speed-the-Plow.* Kopit takes the scatological dialog Mamet is known for and exaggerates it so that in *Nirvana* the dialog is "conducted almost entirely in obscenities."

See SATIRE.

participatory theatre. A type of play in which the audience is involved in the performance. Although Victorian melodrama, with its invitation to the audience to hiss the villain and cheer the hero, was participatory, modern audiences have involved themselves even more fully in the performance of a play. In *Tamara,* created by the Artificial Intelligence Comedy Troupe, spectators join the D'Annunzio family and guests at a villa and choose which cast members to follow through various twists and turns of the plot. One can, for example, hurry upstairs to watch Tamara have hysterics on her bedroom floor, or one can nip smartly along a passageway to observe the rendezvous of the housekeeper and the ballet dancer.

See FOURTH WALL, HAPPENING, MELODRAMA.

passion play. The German equivalent of the English mystery play. Although the plays developed in the same way, the German versions featured comic byplay and horrific devil masks. Attention was mostly on the events of Good Friday. The passion play of Oberammergau, in Bavaria, is world famous and has been performed every ten years, almost without exception, since 1634.

See MYSTERY PLAY.

pastiche. A work patched together from various sources or from various works of a single author. In effect, it parodies the originals. Gerard Alessandrini's *Forbidden Broadway,* which has a new edition each year, uses sketches and musical numbers and pokes fun at various Broadway shows. Charles Busch's *Psycho Beach Party* uses moments from 1960s California beach movies to tell the tale of Chicklet and her surfing pals Star Cat and Kanaka.

See PARODY, REVUE, SATIRE.

pastoral. A drama set in the country and idealizing rustic life. It evolved from Italian pastoral poetry and the eclogue and shepherd's play. The first English pastoral play was John Fletcher's *The Faithful Shepherdess* (1608). Some of Shakespeare's plays contain pastoral episodes: *As You Like It, A Midsummer Night's Dream, Love's Labor's Lost,* and *The Winter's Tale.* Some critics feel that the Renaissance pastoral was an attempt to imitate the satyr plays of Greek classical drama. In their celebration of the joys of country life, Rodgers and Hammerstein's *Oklahoma!,* Frank

Loesser's *Most Happy Fella,* and Simon Gray's *Hidden Laughter* have some elements of the pastoral in them.

See SATYR PLAY.

pathos. The suffering of the hero in classical tragedy and the feelings this engenders in the audience. In Aeschylus' *Prometheus Bound,* the Titan Prometheus is punished by Zeus for defending humans and giving them fire to improve their lives. Prometheus, chained to a rock in a desolate gorge, cries aloud in pain and fear. The audience feels pity and sorrow for the hero. Later these emotions are purged in the katharsis that ends the tragedy.

See CLASSICAL DRAMA, HERO, KATHARSIS.

performance art. A presentation, more often solo than group and highly personal in nature, enhanced by music or art created or finished during the performance, along with slides, films, sound effects, or props. Such performances are often critical of popular culture. *Hajj,* written and directed by Lee Bruer and performed in 1983 by Ruth Malezech, is an hour-long poem during which a woman sits at a vanity table and looks into multiple mirrors, seeing not only her reflection but also her past projected onto screens by closed-circuit television. Filipina-American performance artist Jessica Hagedorn uses her shows to comment on the issues of contemporary Philippine society, and John Kelly and Company, in *Maybe It's Cold Outside,* offers five people playing games in a dormitory.

See MIXED-MEDIA PERFORMANCE.

periaktos. A three-sided prism made of flats and mounted on casters so that it can revolve and show a different background on each. First used in classical Greek theatre and then in the Roman, *periaktoi* are still used as quick-change scenery units.

See FLATS.

period piece. A play from an earlier time, played in the style, costumes, and sets representing the period it depicts. Also, a modern play set in an earlier time and needing historical costumes, for example, Arthur Miller's *The Crucible,* which is set in colonial times. Sometimes the expression "period piece" is used in a disparaging manner to refer to something out-of-date.

See COSTUMES.

peripety, peripeteia. One of the major plot elements in Greek drama, the reversal, usually a reversal in the fortunes of the hero. In a tragedy the hero passes from happiness to misery. In Sophocles' *Ajax,* one of the heroes of the Trojan War, Ajax, seems to have a happy future, but he is so jealous of Odysseus for winning Achilles' armor that he goes mad and eventually kills himself.

The reversal is used in melodrama for surprise. The long-lost brother or fiancé returns just in time to save the heroine from certain death or disgrace. Modern plays, too, use the reversal for comic or romantic effect. In Sandy Wilson's *The Boy Friend,* the delivery boy who loves the penniless girl turns out to be the son of a wealthy family.

See CLASSICAL DRAMA, HERO, MELODRAMA.

periscope ending. A scene at the end of a play that tells what happens to the characters. Arnold Wesker's *Their Very Own and Golden City* offers such a view of his characters' future.

See FLASHBACK, FLASHFORWARD.

persona. The character an actor assumes in a play. Also, the mask an actor wears. In each case it involves the taking on of a personality that is different from that of the actor. Often, the more different the persona is, the more acclaimed the performance. Examples are Laurence Olivier's celebrated performance as Othello and Katherine Helmond's as Bananas in John Guare's *The House of Blue Leaves.*

See MASK.

physical time. The actual time spent watching a play.

See DRAMATIC TIME.

picaresque. Describes an episodic play based on the adventures of a *picaro,* or rogue, that is, an antihero. In Dale Wasserman's *Man of La Mancha,* an actor playing Miguel Cervantes recounts the adventures of his creation, Don Quixote. Roger Miller's *Big River,* a musical adaptation of Mark Twain's *Huckleberry Finn,* details the adventures of Huck and the runaway slave Jim on the Mississippi River.

See ANTIHERO.

picture. The general look of the set as seen from an average seat in the house.

See MISE-EN-SCÈNE.

picture frame. The proscenium arch stage, framed as it is by the wooden arch above and on the sides of the playing area, but having no apron area. The audience looks into the picture that is the play.
See PROSCENIUM ARCH.

Pierrot. A character from the commedia. Also called Pedrolino. He was a *zanni,* or clown servant. His traditional costume was a loose white tunic and full pants, ruff collar, and large white hat with a floppy brim. Sometimes the tunic had large black puffs or buttons down the front, and he always wore white makeup rather than a mask.
See COMMEDIA DELL'ARTE, CLOWN, ZANY.

pin spot. A very narrow spotlight beam, focused on an actor's head. Also called the head spot.
See LIGHTING PLOT, SPOTLIGHT.

pit. In its earliest use, the term refers to the ground floor of a theatre, usually excavated below street level. In Elizabethan playhouses, this area was standing room for the groundlings who bought the cheapest tickets. Now it is the area between the stage and the first row of the house, where the orchestra sits, or the front section of seating, which is called the "orchestra section."
See GROUNDLING, ORKESTRA.

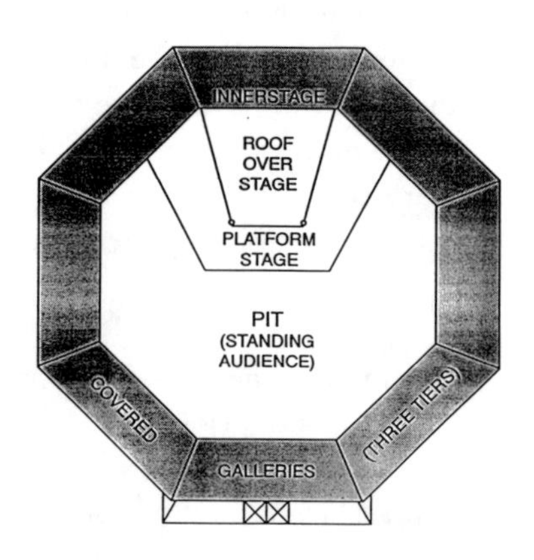

Elizabethan playhouse

pity and fear. The emotions an audience feels for the hero in a tragedy. These emotions are released in the katharsis at the play's end. In Sophocles' *Philoctetes,* the audience pities the suffering of the Trojan War hero marooned on the deserted island of Lemnos with his putrifying wound and his offensive cries of agony, and the audience fears for his sanity and survival.
See HERO, KATHARSIS, TRAGEDY.

plant. The physical property that makes up the theatre complex: playing area, house, scene shop, dressing rooms, grounds, and offices. Also, a person placed in the theatre to lead the laughter, applause, and standing ovation, or placed there to speak lines or contribute to the action of a play. Michael Frayn's *Noises Off* opens with Dotty rehearsing some lines. From the audience, Lloyd corrects her and for some time continues to direct the rehearsal from the house. Also, to foreshadow an event by covertly referring to it early in the play.

See FORESHADOW, PAPERING THE HOUSE.

plastic scenery. Scenery executed in three dimensions rather than just painted on a flat. An example is wooden molding used to trim a wall flat.

See FLAT, SCENERY.

platea. In medieval drama, the playing area in front of a mansion stage. The *platea* provided an extended space for some of the action.

See MANSIONS.

playbill. In the sixteenth century, a small flier given to audiences to announce some details of the production. By the mid-eighteenth century, the playbill had become much larger and included all the information about the play being performed. It became increasingly unwieldy, so by the mid-nineteenth century was reduced in size, eventually becoming what is now the program. The larger playbill became the poster outside the theatre and was displayed on walls as an advertisement.

play of ideas. A play in which the main issue or problem is an intellectual one, such as woman's role in society, class conflict, or the morality of war. Carried to extremes, such a play becomes a windy sermon ignoring the audience-actor relationship. Luigi Pirandello's *Six Characters in Search of an Author* manages to be a play of ideas that also involves characters who engage the audience. As the six characters of the title urge a group of actors to perform their story, the playwright is able to raise questions of appearance versus reality and life versus art.

Henrik Ibsen and George Bernard Shaw also explored social, moral, or philosophical arguments.

See DIDACTIC.

play-within-a-play. A brief play presented during the action of another play. Examples are the artisans' presentation of *Pyramus and Thisbe* in Shakespeare's *A Midsummer Night's Dream,* the party-goers' version of Marivaux's *The Double Constancy* in Jean Anouilh's *The Rehearsal,* and the convicts' presentation of George Farquhar's *The Recruiting Officer* in Timberlake Wertenbaker's *Our Country's Good.* In each case the play-within comments ironically on the play-without.

See DUMB SHOW.

playwright's voice, words. Lines in a play that express the author's feelings on a subject. Early examples can be found in the parabasis of Greek classical comedy in which the chorus came forward to offer the author's views on various subjects. In Aristophanes' *Wasps,* the chorus berates the citizens of Athens for their lack of respect for Aristophanes and in particular for their cool reception of his previous play, *Clouds.*

Recently Arnold Wesker used the character of Beatie in *Roots* to speak for him. In the monolog that closes the play, Beatie scolds her whole social class for not asking questions, for settling for whatever the trash-media offers them, for not caring enough to change things.

See DIDACTIC, PLAY OF IDEAS, RAISONNEUR.

pleasure gardens. Popular in London from the mid-seventeenth century until the late nineteenth century, such gardens offered city dwellers trees and flowers, lawns and paths, band music, dancing, refreshments, a bowling green, a circus, puppet shows, mazes, fireworks, tightrope walkers, and a theatre with farce and vaudeville.

See FARCE, VAUDEVILLE.

plot. **1.** The events of a play; the story as opposed to the theme; what happens rather than what it means. Aristotle maintained that a plot must have unity—that is, each action should initiate the next rather than stand alone without connection to what came before or what follows. In the plot of a play, characters are involved in conflict that has a pattern of entanglement, rising action, crisis, climax, and falling action with resolution. Many romantic plots can be summed up simply as boy meets girl, boy loses girl, boy wins girl.

See ACTION, CLIMAX, CRISIS, DENOUEMENT, ENTANGLEMENT, FALLING ACTION, QUALITATIVE ELEMENTS OF DRAMA, RESOLUTION, RISING ACTION, THEME.

2. A list of lights, properties, and costumes for a particular production. The lighting plot lists the light cues for the lighting technician; the property plot lists all the props needed for a show; the costume plot lists all the costumes worn in a play. The plots, or lists, are arranged by scenes.

See LIGHTING PLOT, PROPERTIES MANAGER, PROPS, WARDROBE MISTRESS.

Plough, Plow Monday. The Monday after Epiphany, or Twelfth Night (January 6). In sixteenth-century England, plays performed on Plough Monday rivaled the mummers' plays of Christmas in popularity. In the plough plays the characters were not heroes like St. George or Robin Hood, but farmhands, and the chief incident was a death by accident, not in battle. Like the mummers' play, the plough play was probably a survivor of primitive folk festivals.

See MUMMERS.

***Poetics*.** Aristotle's treatise on the nature of art. He used tragedy as his example of drama throughout because he considered it the highest, most perfect form of art. In the *Poetics,* Aristotle covers such topics as the genesis of tragedy and its qualitative elements.

See AESTHETICS, QUALITATIVE ELEMENTS OF DRAMA, TRAGEDY.

point of attack. The moment in a play at which the main action of the plot begins. This may occur in the first scene, as in Shakespeare's *Othello,* when Iago, filled with hatred because Othello has denied him a promotion, promises to "serve my turn upon him." Or it may occur after several scenes of exposition, as in Eugene O'Neill's *Desire Under the Elms,* when Ephraim Cabot brings home his third wife. Often the point of attack is just such an arrival of a new and major character: Blanche in Tennessee Williams's *A Streetcar Named Desire,* Anna in O'Neill's *Anna Christie,* and Finian and his daughter Sharon in E. Y. Harburg's *Finian's Rainbow.*

See INCITING INCIDENT.

poor theatre. A term coined by director Jerzy Grotowski for the experimental work he did in the 1950s and 1960s with the Polish Laboratory Theatre. The basic concept was that theatre must be poor, that is, stripped of all that is not essential—no illusionary lighting effects, no makeup, no costuming, no realistic settings, and no music other than that which the actors themselves create. In this way, Grotowski felt, nothing could deflect the actor's relationship with the audience.

See AVANT-GARDE.

portfolio. A folder containing photographs, a resume, reviews, and other evidence of a performer's work, assembled for presentation at interviews with prospective employers. A technician's portfolio would include sketches and photographs of set designs, costume designs, advertising campaigns, and so on, rather than personal photographs.

practical scenery. Scenery that actually works on stage—a stove that cooks, cupboards that open and hold things, books that can be read, a tap that runs water, a window that opens. In Willy Russell's *Shirley Valentine,* the solo character peels, slices, and fries potatoes on a stove. In Robert Harling's *Steel Magnolias,* M'Lynn's hair is shampooed under a tap, and in Alan Ayckbourn's *Man of the Moment,* a character drowns in a swimming pool.

precast. To cast certain roles in a production before the auditions are held.

See AUDITION.

premiere. The first public performance of a play. Although the play may have had workshop productions and even preview performances, the official opening night is considered the premiere.

presentational. A style of performance in which the actors recognize and address the audience, in contrast to representational style in which the actors observe the convention of a fourth wall. The address to the audience may be a simple aside, as in Renaissance plays or Victorian melodrama. Or it may be a soliloquy, such as Helena's in *All's Well That Ends Well* when she reads aloud and reacts to Bertram's letter abandoning her. The address to the audience may be a chorus in a Greek tragedy, providing exposition for the audience, or a chorus character narrating events, as does Styles the photographer in Athol Fugard, John Kani, and Winston Ntshonas's *Sizwe Banzi Is Dead.* Or it may be a character who addresses the audience throughout, as does the domineering schoolteacher in Roberto Athayde's *Miss*

Margarida's Way.

See FOURTH WALL, REPRESENTATIONAL.

preset. An arrangement of the lighting board controls prepared in advance of its need. With computerized lighting boards, each scene's lighting cues can be preset.

See LIGHTING PLOT.

primary colors. In stage lighting, any shade of color can be produced by blending varied amounts of the three primary colors—blue, red, and green. When these primary colors, each one from a different light source, are blended in equal amounts, white light is produced. In scene painting, the primary colors are cyan (bluish green), yellow, and magenta (bluish red). These primary colors can be mixed in paints to produce any shade of color.

principal boy. In English panto, the hero, who is always played by a pretty girl in a blonde wig, short tunic, flesh-colored tights, and high heels. In the 1970s Linda Thorsen played Dandini in *Cinderella,* and Barbara Windsor played the title role in *Aladdin.*

See PANTOMIME, PANTS PART.

principals. The leading characters in a play; the leading actors in a company. Some rehearsals are held just for the principals. In Edmund Rostand's *Cyrano de Bergerac,* Cyrano, Christian, and Roxanne are the principals. However, some critics consider only the protagonist to be the principal, in this case Cyrano, the one around whom the plot revolves.

See HERO, PROTAGONIST, STOCK COMPANY.

prior life. The presumed life of a character before his or her appearance in a play. In preparing a role, an actor must assemble all the clues in the script then flesh out the details with imagination and research into time and place. To help develop a characterization, an actor may need to decide what the character's relationships with his parents were, his favorite color, and whether the character had a pet as a child, and maybe even what kind.

problem play. Any play that deals with the problems of life, such as thwarted young love in *Romeo and Juliet* or tyranny in Christopher Marlowe's *Tamburlaine,* is a problem play. More commonly, a problem play is one that explores a particular social or psychological problem that confronts the protagonist. Examples are G. B. Shaw's *Major Barbara,* Henrik Ibsen's *A Doll's House,* and J. B. Priestley's *An Inspector Calls.*

See PLAY OF IDEAS.

producer. The person who puts together a theatrical production: obtains financial backing; leases the rights to the play; rents the theatre; hires the director, designers, house and stage crews; supervises the advertising and budget; and, sometimes, hires the cast. In England the term *producer* is often used for what in America is called the director. Noted producers include Emanuel Azenberg *(The Real Thing),* Cheryl Crawford (of the Actors' Studio), Fran Weissler *(Gypsy),* and Elizabeth I. McCann (63 Tony nominations).

See DIRECTOR, MANAGER.

projection. Use of a projector like a Linnebach (a socket and lamp inside a black box with guides for the slide to be projected) to throw images onto a cyclorama or the back wall of a set. The images may be static or moving, such as clouds.

See GOBO, VOICE PROJECTION.

prologue. In Greek tragedy, the action before the entrance of the chorus. In Euripides' *Medea,* it is the Nurse's lament that Jason ever came to Colchis and caused Medea to love him. Since that time, a prologue has meant a speech to introduce a play. Later examples include the prologue spoken by Horner in William Wycherley's *The Country Wife* and the exposition provided by the chorus of women at the start of T. S. Eliot's *Murder in the Cathedral.*

See EPILOG.

prompt book. The stage manager's copy of the script in which are noted all the blocking and technical cues. This is prepared by the stage manager in the course of rehearsal or in advance by the director.

See CUE, STAGE MANAGER.

prompt corner. The area just behind the proscenium arch at stage left where the prompter sits with the prompt book. Thus the stage designation *P.C.* means the prompt side or stage left, while *O.P.* means opposite the prompt side or stage right.

See CUE, SIT ON BOOK.

propaganda play. A play dealing with a political or social issue and proposing a solution. G. B. Shaw's *Pygmalion* asserts that differing dialects reinforce the class structure of society. David Rabe's *The Basic Training of Pavlo Hummel* deals with war and Shelagh Delaney's *A Taste of Honey,* with family problems.

See DIDACTIC, GUERRILLA THEATRE, PLAY OF IDEAS, PROBLEM PLAY.

properties manager. The person responsible for acquiring all the props needed for a play, placing them where they belong on the set, handing them to the actors as needed to take onstage, getting them back again after a performance, and creating offstage effects as called for by the script. The term is often abbreviated to "prop man."

This is a very important job since the wrong prop can bring the play to a halt, as when an actor in William Saroyan's *The Time of Your Life* brought on a bag of toys in a scene where he should have brought on a bag of chewing gum. There was no gum to chew and comment on in the lines that followed. Some shows require few props, but George Kaufman and Moss Hart's *You Can't Take It With You* has a prop plot of over three hundred items.

See PLOT.

props. Short for stage properties. These are usually divided into four categories: hand props—those carried onstage or handled by the actors (fans, letters, glasses); set or scene props—large items placed on the floor (furniture, rugs, statuary, rocks, bushes); dress props—things that trim the set (pictures, curtains, wall sconces, mirrors); and effects not produced in the lighting booth (doorbells, knocking, crashes, smoke, wind, fog). Although occasional arguments may develop over whether a sword is costume or prop, most crews abide by the above designations.

Props are pulled from company stock, bought, rented, borrowed, or fabricated. Fabricated props include food sculpted from cold mashed potatoes, candy-glass mirrors (to be broken), breakaway chairs, and foliage made of wire and fabric.

See EFFECTS.

proscenium arch. The picture frame through which an audience watches the play in a proscenium arch theatre. Architecturally, it comprises the wooden lintel and sidepieces that enclose the playing area. Immediately behind the front or house curtain is the inner proscenium, which consists of a horizontal drape across the top, called the "teaser," and floor-length side drapes called "tormentors."

See PICTURE FRAME, TEASER, TORMENTOR.

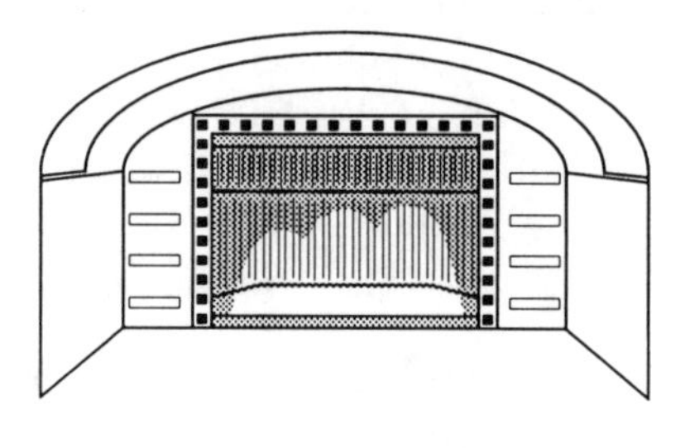

Proscenium arch

proskenium. In Greek classical drama, the facade of the skene building, painted to represent the setting of the play in performance.

See SKENE.

protagonist. From the Greek *protos,* meaning "first." In Greek drama the chief, and at first the only, actor in a play. Now it means the principal character around whom the action revolves. He or she is a dynamic character whose conflict provides the plot of the play. Some examples are the title characters in Shakespeare's *Pericles* and Simon Gray's *Butley.*

See ACTION, ANTAGONIST, CONFLICT, DYNAMIC CHARACTER, HERO.

psychodrama. A kind of participatory theatre in which players are not actors and do not follow a script. Instead, they provide, or are provided with, a hypothetical or autobiographical problem and then improvise a solution or at least explore the possibilities. If the problem is an autobiographical one, the director, often a therapist, may ask a player to take the part of his or her antagonist, in order to see the problem from an opposing point of view. Those taking part may be parents and child, husband and wife, or other family members.

Psychodrama is also used in crisis intervention workshops. The players are actors or volunteers who play out a prepared scenario dealing with a potential crisis—a distraught student, an enraged employee, or anyone who might precipitate a crisis situation. In the course of the action, spectators try to develop ways of handling the situation. Psychodrama is more therapeutic than artistic in its intentions.

Pulitzer Prize. One of several literary prizes awarded according to the will of Joseph Pulitzer (1847–1911). In drama the prize is given to the "best American play performed in New York," generally one showing the power and educational value of the theatre. The prize was awarded first in 1918 to Jesse Lynch Williams for *Why Marry?* Eugene O'Neill won it four times. George Kaufman won in 1932 for *Of Thee I Sing,* William Saroyan in 1940 for *The Time of Your Life,* Charles Gordone in 1970 for *No Place to Be Somebody,* and Neil Simon in 1991 for *Lost in Yonkers.*

Punch and Judy show. A hand-puppet show, usually given in a park or fair, operated by one person in a booth the top half of which is the stage. Punch and Judy are married and quarrel constantly. Punch wears a striped coat and has a huge hook nose and a humpback. He behaves violently, throwing the baby out the window, beating Judy and the other characters, and even winning a battle with the Devil, all in a manner meant to amuse rather than frighten the children watching. A dog, the faithful Toby, sits at the side, wearing a wide ruff collar and observing throughout.

Punchinello. One of the comic servant characters of the commedia. He is a humpbacked, stupid fellow who probably evolved from the *Maccus* of the *fabula atellana.* In England he became the Punch of Punch and Judy shows.

See COMMEDIA DELL'ARTE, FABULA ATELLANA, PUNCH AND JUDY SHOW.

purchase line. The rope held by a member of the stage crew to fly the scenery in a counterweight system.

See COUNTERWEIGHT, FLY, SCENERY.

qualitative elements of drama. Aristotle believed that drama (tragedy) could be analyzed not only in its quantitative elements—that is, the chronological development from prologue to *exodos*—but also in its qualitative elements—that is, the logical development of six aspects: plot, thought, character, diction, music, and spectacle. He placed plot first because he said dramas were not mere character studies but must also arouse pity and fear and then purge the audience of those emotions. He placed thought next but said it must be subordinate to action. Character and diction rank next and music and spectacle are last.

See CHARACTER, CLASSICAL DRAMA, DICTION, MUSIC, PLOT, POETICS, THOUGHT, TRAGEDY, SPECTACLE.

raison d'être. French, meaning "reason for being." In a play it is the reason behind a character's words or actions.

See MOTIVATION.

raisonneur. A kind of chorus character, generally on the periphery of the action, who speaks the views of the playwright. In G. B. Shaw's *You Never Can Tell,* the waiter William explains that it's the unexpected that always happens, and so you never can tell.

See CHORUS CHARACTER, PLAYWRIGHT'S VOICE.

rake. In eighteenth- and nineteenth-century theatres, the angle of incline from downstage to upstage. Originally, this promoted the illusion of perspective in the scenery.

reader's theatre. A performance at which a play is read aloud for an audience rather than memorized and presented off book. In reader's theatre the actors may dress alike or may dress in costume; they may sit on stools or stand at lecterns or walk about the stage. The play script is usually held in a folder and, although the play has been rehearsed and the actors are familiar with the lines, there is no attempt to pretend they are not reading.

A second kind of reader's theatre involves a group of people who meet to read aloud a play for themselves and a few friends. There is no rehearsal and parts may not even be assigned until the meeting. Often the reading is followed by a discussion of the work.

Plays that are often presented as reader's theatre are *Under Milkwood* by Dylan Thomas, *John Brown's Body* by Stephen Vincent Benét, *Don Juan in Hell* by G. B. Shaw, and *Spoon River Anthology* by Edgar Lee Masters.

realism. An attempt in theatre to represent everyday life and people as they are or appear to be, through careful attention to detail in motivation of characters, costuming, setting, and dialog. However, unlike naturalism, realism need not adhere to a philosophy of pessimistic determinism. The movement toward realism began at the end of the nineteenth century with Henrik Ibsen, who greatly influenced G. B. Shaw and Anton Chekhov. Realism spread rapidly and demanded a new type of acting to interpret the plays. This led to the development of the Stanislavsky method of actors' training.

In *A Streetcar Named Desire* by Tennessee Williams, the script calls for such realistic details as a plaster statuette of Mae West that Mitch wins at an amusement park, Stanley's loud silk bowling shirt, poker chips, playing cards, bare light bulbs, a candle stub in a wine bottle, and the pork chops Stanley holds in his hand to gnaw. The violent and vulgar speech Williams provides for Stanley brings out the character's brutal nature.

See NATURALISM.

recognition scene. The moment in a play when a character who has long been away is recognized, or some information that was withheld from a character is revealed.

See ANAGNORISIS.

reflector. A hood of polished metal, shaped into a sphere, a parabola, or an ellipsoid, with a light source at its center. The light is augmented when it hits the reflecting surface. The reflector may be used with both spotlight and floodlight.

See FLOODLIGHT, PAR, SPOTLIGHT.

regional theatre. Also called resident theatre. A professional, nonprofit theatre located away from such major theatre centers as Broadway.

There are more than seventy regional theatres in this country, providing more than six hundred productions a year of standard as well as new plays. Among those recognized as outstanding are South Coast Repertory in Costa Mesa, Calif.; Guthrie Theatre in Minneapolis; Goodman Theatre in Chicago; and Alley Theatre in Houston.

See REPERTORY COMPANY.

rehearsal. A session in which the director and actors prepare a play for performance.

See BLOCKING, DIRECTOR, DRESS REHEARSAL, RUN-THROUGH, TECH REHEARSAL.

relation to characters. An establishment of relationships in a play so that actors who play characters connected by blood, marriage, friendship, or conflict will act as though they have been involved in actual relationships and will not give the impression they just met in rehearsal.

relation to objects. An establishment of relationships in a play so that actors using certain objects or wearing certain clothes will act as if these items are really theirs and not as if they saw the objects or garments for the first time in rehearsal. For example, in G. B. Shaw's *Candida,* Prosperine should take a proprietary interest in her typewriter, not only being thoroughly familiar with its operation but also being genuinely annoyed with Marchbanks for having tinkered with it.

repertoire. All the parts an actor has played, or all the plays he or she is familiar with. Also, the plays in production by a company in a single season, or the plays the company knows well enough to present on short notice. In a single season, for example, the Dallas (Tex.) Theatre Center offered a repertoire of *Farce and Flick, Fantoccini, Hamlet ESP, Peter Pan, The Seagull, Harvey, The Night Thoreau Spent in Jail, The Apple Tree, Private Lives, The Late Christopher Bean, Waiting for Godot, Anna Christie, Dear Liar, The Attendant,* and *The Diary of a Madman.*

repertory company. A theatre group that performs the plays in the season's repertoire, with members taking large parts in some plays and small parts in others, and some members, especially apprentices, having technical responsibilities. Some repertory companies are the Royal Shakespeare Company in Stratford, England; Berkeley (Calif.)

Repertory; Missouri Repertory in Kansas City; and Trinity Repertory in Providence, R.I.

representational. A style of acting in which the convention of a fourth wall is maintained and actors do not address or mingle with the audience. Also, a style of production that seeks to create the illusions of an actual room on stage.

See FOURTH WALL, PRESENTATIONAL.

resolution. The moment at which the conflict in a play is resolved.

See DENOUEMENT.

Restoration drama. Drama written and performed during the Restoration when the House of Stuart returned to the throne of England. Although Charles II reigned from 1660 to 1685, the Restoration period in drama is considered to be from 1660 to 1700. Although heroic and neoclassical tragedies were also produced, the period is especially known for the comedy of manners that mocks the pretender, the fop, the old man who marries a young wife, and the old woman trying to be young. Women appeared on the English stage for the first time, resulting in expanded roles. Popular plays of the time were *The Man of Mode* by George Etherege, *The Beaux' Stratagem* by George Farquhar, and *The Country Wife* by William Wycherley.

One of the humorous devices employed in Restoration comedy was naming the characters in a way that described them: Fainall, Wilfull Witwound, Petulant, Waitwell, and Foible are characters in William Congreve's *The Way of the World;* Pinchwife, in *The Country Wife;* and Sir Fopling Flutter, in *The Man of Mode.*

See COMEDY OF MANNERS, HEROIC DRAMA, NEOCLASSICISM.

return. Two flats hinged together to fold outward, back-to-back. Because they open away from the audience, they may serve to mask offstage areas. Also, a downstage flat, parallel to the back wall and running off into the wings just upstage of the tormentor, or acting as a tormentor.

See FLAT, MASK, TORMENTOR.

revenge play. Any play about bloody retribution. Specifically, the plays of sixteenth- and seventeenth-century England in which the protagonist attempts to avenge himself or herself on a villain.

See JACOBEAN REVENGE TRAGEDY.

reversal. A plot reversal when an action produces the opposite of what was desired or expected.

See PERIPETY.

review. The announcement in print or broadcast media of a production with some description of the cast, plot, and technical aspects. Although the review may offer an opinion, it is not generally considered a piece of serious criticism. However, since a favorable review can make a show a success and a negative one can finish a play, those involved in a production generally take reviews seriously. It is the practice to quote from good reviews in press releases and in paid advertisements for a play.

See CRITICISM.

revival. A play performed sometime after its original production. There is a category in the Tony Awards for revivals. Perennial favorites for revival are the plays of Shakespeare, Molière, G. B. Shaw, Henrik Ibsen, Anton Chekhov, Oscar Wilde, Noel Coward, Tennessee Williams, Eugene O'Neill, Arthur Miller, and Alan Ayckbourn, and such musicals as *Fiddler on the Roof, Hello Dolly, Gypsy,* and *Anything Goes.* To be a true revival, the production should be a faithful recreation of the original; otherwise, it should be called an adaptation or a new version.

See TONY AWARDS.

revolve. A revolving stage. It may be a permanent, electrically driven turntable or a temporary portable—that is, a large circular wagon with a pivot point at its center. Scenery is mounted on it and as it is rotated it presents different settings to the audience.

revue. A production featuring a collection of songs, dances, or sketches. These may have a narrative thread, share a theme, be from the work of one person, or follow no particular sequence. The nonmusical revue, such as *Beyond the Fringe* by Alan Bennett, Jonathan Miller, Peter Cook, and Dudley Moore, often presents sketches of a topical or satirical nature. Arthur Arent and Harold Rome's *Pins and Needles* (1937) regularly changed its material to reflect the national and international politics of the time. Famous revue series include the *Ziegfeld Follies, George White Scandals, Earl Carroll's Vanities,* and Steve Silver's *Beach Blanket Babylon.*

See EXTRAVAGANZA, SKETCH.

rigging. The process of hanging scenery or lights; the handling of the stage curtain or drops. Also, the complete system of ropes, blocks, and pins for manipulating scenery.

See DROP, SCENERY, STAGE CREW.

rising action. That portion of the plot beginning with the inciting incident and proceeding to the climax, with the action increasing in intensity and excitement. In Harold Pinter's *The Caretaker,* from the moment Mick enters the room, knocks the tramp Davies to the floor, and then breaks the horrified silence to demand, "What's the game?," the tension increases until Davies is foolish enough to take sides with Mick against Aston. Then the audience realizes that it is just such a betrayal that will finish Davies with Mick and Aston. The tramp's poor judgment puts him in the brothers' power and he is reduced to begging to be allowed to stay.

See CLIMAX, FALLING ACTION, INCITING INCIDENT.

ritual. A prescribed form or ceremony. Drama began in religious ritual and now, because ritual provides structure, much present-day drama attempts to develop new rituals or revise old ones. The Performance Group's *Dionysus in 69* included a birth ritual adopted from Asmat New Guinea ceremonies. Jean Genet's *The Blacks* shows a troupe of black performers reenacting the ritual killing of a white woman, and Jerzy Grotowski's *The Constant Prince,* which is a free adaptation of Pedro Calderone's seventeenth-century play, suggests the crucifixion of Christ in its depiction of the anguish and death of the prince.

See AVANT-GARDE, DIONYSIAN, MEDIEVAL DRAMA.

road company. A group of actors who take a show on the road, performing short runs at a series of towns. The company may include the stars who created the leading roles on Broadway.

See BARNSTORMING, BUS AND TRUCK COMPANY.

role. Part in a play; the character played by an actor in a play.

See CHARACTER.

Roman drama. Begun in 350 B.C. with a solo performer accompanied by a flute, Roman drama enjoyed its golden age from 240 to 204 B.C. It then declined until all theatrical performances were banned by Emperor Justinian in the sixth century A.D.

In its heyday, Roman drama was produced at public festivals by state companies of actors—mostly slaves or freedmen. There were comedies and tragedies, both showing Greek influence and enhanced with dancing, juggling, acrobatics, and flute accompaniment. Although there was no speaking chorus, there was a vocal choir. The audience included all classes, men and women. The physical plant had a proscenium arch, wings, and a semicircular house. If there was a curtain, it was lowered into a trench to start and then raised at the conclusion. There was conventional costuming: red for slave characters, yellow for courtesans. All the action took place on a set that depicted the outdoors, usually a street before two or three houses. The action was continuous with no act or scene divisions. The acting was highly stylized with stock characters, and masks and wigs were worn. Since the performances took place in daylight, there were no lighting effects. An exit to the left meant a character was going to foreign parts; to the right meant the nearby countryside. Performances used asides, soliloquies, and eavesdropping, and there were frequent violations of dramatic illusion for comic effect, such as the character of a slave who delivers asides about one of the other characters.

The major writers of Roman comedy were Plautus *(Amphitryon, Menaechmi)* and Terence *(Eunuchus, Phormio)*; of tragedy, Seneca *(Medea, Trojan Women)*.

See ANGIPORTUM, CONVENTION, FABULA ATELLANA, STOCK CHARACTERS.

romanticism. A nineteenth-century tendency toward florid staging of the grand passions of larger-than-life characters. It survives today in grand opera and, to a lesser degree, in romantic comedy in which the central plot concerns a love affair between an idealized hero and heroine. The affair does not run smoothly, but it ends happily. Examples are William Inge's *Picnic,* Lerner and Loewe's *Brigadoon,* and Shakespeare's *The Merchant of Venice.*

See INGENUE, JUVENILE.

royalty. The payment made to a playwright for permission to perform his or her play. Royalties were first paid in the eighteenth century but were not uniformly recognized until this century.

See COPYRIGHT.

run lines. To recite the lines of a play without the accompanying blocking or stage business. This is often done to help actors get off book.
See OFF BOOK, LINES.

run of the play. The length of time a play is presented in a series of consecutive performances.

run-through. A rehearsal at which an entire scene, act, or play is done without stopping for changes or corrections.
See REHEARSAL.

runway. A narrow extension of the stage running out into the audience. It may be horseshoe-shaped around the orchestra pit or T-shaped down the center of the house. Performers in burlesque and revues use the runway for musical numbers. The ramp on which the "train" race is skated in *Starlight Express* by Andrew Lloyd Webber and Tim Rice is a runway.
See BURLESQUE, REVUE.

safety curtain. A fireproof sheet of heavy fabric that can be lowered in front of the house curtain in a proscenium arch. The first safety curtain was installed in a London theatre, the Drury Lane, in 1794.

See ASBESTOS CURTAIN, HOUSE CURTAIN, PROSCENIUM ARCH.

sandbag. A canvas bag filled with sand and used as a counterweight for a scenery flying system.

See COUNTERWEIGHT SYSTEM, FLYING, PURCHASE LINE.

satire. A type of comedy that uses wit, irony, and exaggeration to expose individual and institutional folly, vice, and stupidity. Satire aims, directly or indirectly, at correcting such abuses. It may be Horatian (after Horace, a Latin poet of the first century B.C.)—that is, gentle, humorous, and urbane. G. B. Shaw's *Arms and the Man* mocks the romanticizing of war through the character of Bluntschli, the "chocolate cream soldier," who knows it is better to carry food than bullets in his holster. Or satire may be Juvenalian (after Juvenal, a Roman satirist of the first century A.D.)—that is, biting and sarcastic. Barbara Garson's *MacBird* attempts to draw a parallel between Macbeth and President Lyndon Johnson.

See DIDACTICISM, PARODY.

saturna. An early Italian preliterary performance consisting of music, mime, and dialog.

See FABULA ATELLANA, FESCENNINE VERSES, MIME.

satyr play. Comic skits that followed the tragedy trilogies in ancient Athens, often commenting rudely on them and providing comic relief. In the satyr plays a heroic figure, such as Hercules, and a chorus of half-man, half-animal satyrs were involved in fast action, energetic dancing or capering about, boisterous antics, and vulgar jokes. Although they share the same Greek root, the word *satyr* should not be confused with *satire.* The only complete surviving satyr play is Euripides' *The Cyclops,* but fragments of Sophocles' *The Trackers* were found in 1907 and published in 1912, and a reconstruction of the play by English poet Tony Harrison was recently staged at the National Theatre in London.

See CLASSICAL DRAMA, TETRALOGY, TRILOGY.

scaena. The Roman equivalent of the Greek *skene* or dressing rooms for actors.

See SKENE.

scaena ductilis. In Roman theatre, a moving backdrop, probably a painted canvas on rollers.

scaffold. Another term for the mansion of medieval theatre. A specific setting for a scene.

See MANSIONS, PLATEA.

Scapino. One of the *zanni,* or clown servants, of the commedia. His character was crafty and prone to scamper off—as his name suggests—if things got out of hand. He was a liar and a ladies' man, and he always dressed in green-and-white stripes. The character evolved into the rascally valet in Molière's *Les Fourberies de Scapin.*

See COMEDIA DELL'ARTE.

Scaramuccia, Scaramouche. A commedia character, sometimes a braggart soldier, sometimes a clown servant. He loves women and wine and is always dressed in black.

See COMMEDIA DELL'ARTE.

scenario. A film or television script. Originally a scenario was a scene-by-scene resume of the plot in a commedia play. This provided a skeleton that could be fleshed out in performance by the inventiveness of the actors.

See COMMEDIA DELL'ARTE.

scene. A division of an act or of the play itself (some plays are not divided into acts). The scene division may be dictated by a change of time or place in the play and is signaled to the audience by lowering the curtain or briefly darkening the stage, often with accompanying mood music.

The term is also sometimes used to mean the setting, as in, "The scene is laid in New York City."

See ACT.

scène à faire. A scene the audience expects.

See OBLIGATORY SCENE.

scenery. The background forms—walls, archways, sky, trees, skyline, stairs—that provide the setting for a play. This may be a box set representing the room of a house, a cyclorama painted sky blue, suspended archways, or a painted backdrop of mountains. The scenery designer sketches the setting and the construction crew executes the design. The basic unit of scenery construction is the flat; several flats joined together constitute a set. Scenery is one of the elements in the total look of a play.

See ABSTRACT SET, ARRAS SETTING, BACKDROP, BOX SET, CURTAIN SET, DETAIL SCENERY, FLAT, FLY(ING), FULL SCENERY, GREEK IT, GROUND CLOTH, JACKKNIFE, LASH LINES, MANSIONS, MASK, MINIMAL SETTING, MISE-EN-SCÈNE, MULTIPLE SETTINGS, PLASTIC SCENERY, PRACTICAL SCENERY, RETURN, REVOLVE, RIGGING, SCAFFOLD, SCENE SHOP, SCRIM, SET DESIGNER, SHOW PORTAL, SIGHT LINES, SKY DROP, STRIKE THE SET, SURROUND, TEASER, TORMENTOR, UNIT SET, WAGON, WILD.

scene shop, bay, dock. The shop is the area where scenery is built and painted, where materials and tools are stored, and where a setting can be assembled on a trial basis. The scene bay is an area immediately offstage where scenery can be stored. The scene dock is the landing immediately outside the scene shop where large elements of scenery—stair units and shrouds—can be stored.

schmaltz. Sentimental material or sentimental treatment of material, such as in Claude-Michel Schönberg and Alain Boublil's *Miss Saigon.* The term *schmaltz* also refers to overacting in a serious piece so that the performance is maudlin and corny.

See SENTIMENTAL COMEDY.

scrim. A dark-blue theatrical gauze sturdier than commercial gauze. One or more thicknesses of it are hung as a drop in front of a scene. With the careful control of light, a variety of effects are possible. With no light at all thrown onto the scrim, it remains invisible but the objects behind it are seen as if in a mist. A few streaks of light thrown across the scrim produce an effect of fog. A scene can be played in front of the scrim and then the scrim lifted to reveal another setting already in place.

See SCENERY.

second banana. The stooge of the lead comic in a show, sometimes his confidant, but always the butt of his jokes. The term derives from an old burlesque routine about the distribution of a bunch of bananas between the lead comic and his assistant.

See BURLESQUE, CONFIDANT, VICE.

sense memory. An actor's device for summoning up emotion by recalling a previous real-life event.

See AFFECTIVE MEMORY, EMOTIONAL RECALL, METHOD ACTING.

sentimental comedy. An eighteenth-century reaction to the immorality expressed in Restoration comedy. Richard Steele is regarded as the leading writer of the type. His plays include *The Tender Husband* and *The Conscious Lovers.* Sentimental comedy lacked humor, reality, and a light touch. The characters were all-good or all-bad, becoming caricatures, and the plots were wrenched to have virtue always triumph.

See SCHMALTZ.

Serlian wing. Permanent set pieces used in pairs to create perspective, as a line of trees or houses fading into the distance. First described by Italian painter and architect Sebastiano Serlio in *De architettura* (1545), a treatise on architecture.

set designer. The person responsible for designing and overseeing the construction of a stage setting. He or she must take into consideration the needs of the play, the blocking of the actors, the director's vision of the piece, the type of stage to be used, and the budget. The set must be designed to establish and maintain mood, time, and place. It must also maintain the characterization of the occupant of the room represented and reinforce the theme.

See MISE-EN-SCÈNE, SET(TING), STAGE CREW.

set piece. A scene from a play that can be performed out of context and still make sense. Set pieces include the scene in which Cleopatra and Caesar first meet at the Sphinx in G. B. Shaw's *Caesar and Cleopatra,* the scene in Noel Coward's *Private Lives* in which Amanda and Elyot find themselves on the balcony of the same hotel on their separate honeymoons, and the scene from Anton Chekhov's *Uncle Vanya* in which Astroff shows Elena the charts of the countryside he has made.

set(ting). The surroundings in which the action of a play develops. Also, the units of scenery that combine to suggest a particular place.

See SCENERY.

sharp focus. The narrowest beam of light from a stage light.

shoe. Protective framing for furniture legs, used by touring companies.

showcase. A presentation designed to show off the ability of a particular actor or group of actors. Also, the theatre offering such presentations. Producers and agents are invited so they can appraise the work of those being showcased. The run may be as short as one performance. The actors may be just getting started in the theatre or may be trying to break away from typecasting by acting in pieces different from what they are known for. California School of the Arts in Valencia rents a Los Angeles theatre each spring to showcase its graduating company. Each student performs a monolog and a scene.

See EQUITY WAIVER HOUSE, TYPECASTING.

show portal. A system of a framed teaser and tormentors built especially for a particular show.

See TEASER, TORMENTOR.

shroud. The portable platforms that surround a revolve or turntable.
See REVOLVE.

shtick, shtik. A piece of stage business, usually designed for a quick and easy laugh. Sometimes it catches on with an audience and becomes part of the actor's repertoire. But an actor who relies on shtick instead of acting may play a part without ever becoming the character.
See BUSINESS, MUGGING.

shutters. Sheets of metal or opaque material, mounted in the color frame slide of a spotlight, used to shape or reduce the beam of light projected.
See GOBO, MAT.

sides. Portions of a script containing one actor's lines and cues.
See SPEECHES.

sight lines. Imaginary lines from the audience to the stage. Set designers must consider these so that people on the extreme sides of the house are able to see important areas on either side of the stage. Directors also must plan the blocking to accommodate sight lines and ensure that offstage areas are masked from every spot in the house.
See BLOCKING, MASKING, SET DESIGNER.

site specific. A play or sketch created to be performed in a particular place. The En Garde Arts Company's *Father Was a Peculiar Man* was written for and performed in the meat-packing district of New York City.

sit on book. To prompt actors in rehearsal by feeding them their lines when they call out, "Line."
See OFF, ON BOOK.

sizing. A preparation used to fill in the pores of a surface. Sizing on flats and drops is used to prevent excessive paint absorption. To *size* means to preshrink fabric that is to be painted.
See DROP, FLAT.

skene. In classical Greek theatre, the building immediately behind the *proskeniun* that contained dressing rooms for the actors. It had side wings jutting out past the *proskeniun* and on top there was a platform called the *theologeion* from where heroes or gods could speak during the course of the play.

See PROSKENIUN, SCAENA.

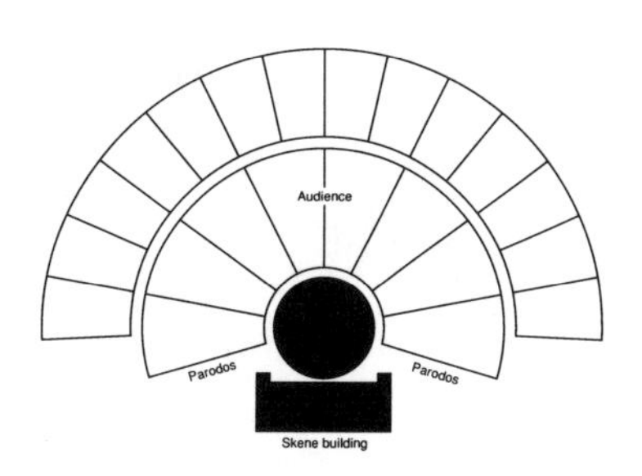

Greek theatre

sketch. A short piece or skit, complete in itself, that is presented within a longer work, such as a revue, vaudeville, or burlesque performance. A sketch lacks the plot development or deep characterizations possible in longer works, but can serve to make a point and entertain. In George C. Wolfe's *The Colored Museum,* a revue that provides a look at "contemporary African-American values," one of the sketches concerns two high-fashion wigs arguing over which one their owner will wear that night.

See BURLESQUE, REVUE, VAUDEVILLE.

sky drop. A backdrop painted to represent the sky.

See BACKDROP, DROP.

slapstick. Literally, two hinged wooden slats attached to a handle. When the device strikes a person, a loud smack is heard. Originally used by Harlequin in commedia *lazzi.* The term now refers to any comedy that features physical, often abusive, pranks.

See LAZZO, LOW COMEDY.

slice of life. Naturalistic drama purporting to offer a direct presentation of reality without selection or arrangement. *The Weavers* (1892) by the German dramatist Gerhart Hauptmann is an early example of this style. More recently, there have been experiments in which a group of actors or a family lived on stage for a period of time and spectators could drop in and observe for as long as they liked.

See NATURALISM.

small work. Subtle facial expressions and gestures used to illuminate character. Called "eyelash and fingernail acting" by playwright Alan Ayckbourn, these actions seldom appear in the stage directions or are even specified by the director. Instead, they arise organically out of an actor's understanding of the role. For example, an actor playing Beatrice in Arthur Miller's *A View from the Bridge* might continually pleat and then smooth the fabric of her skirt as she reluctantly tells her niece that she must start her own life, away from Beatrice and her husband.

See BUSINESS, DECORUM, IN THE MOMENT.

soccus. The low-heeled slipper or sandal worn by the actors in Greek comedy.

See BUSKIN.

social comedy. Plays that deal satirically with society's manners and mores. Anna Cora Mowatt Richie's *Fashion* (1845) set the style for American social comedies.

See COMEDY OF MANNERS, RESTORATION DRAMA.

soliloquy. A speech in which an actor, usually alone on stage, speaks his or her thoughts aloud. The most famous is Hamlet's, which begins,"To be or not to be. . . ." Other memorable soliloquies are Macbeth's "Tomorrow, and tomorrow, and tomorrow. . . ." and Othello's "It is the cause, it is the cause, my soul. . . ."

See ASIDE, CONVENTION.

soubrette. The vivacious, pert, usually comic female, often the confidante of the ingenue, and the actor who plays such roles. The soubrettes of commedia were frolicsome country girls or saucy serving maids. They were full-figured, dressed in peasant garb with a large apron and hair bow. Their names were Francheschina, Coralina, and Columbina.

In modern theatre, soubrettes are found in such musicals as *Oklahoma!* (Ado Annie), *Most Happy Fella* (Cleo), *Guys and Dolls* (Adelaide), and *West Side Story* (Anita).

See CONFIDANT, INGENUE.

spear carrier. Slang expression for an actor who appears on stage just to fill out a crowd or procession. The term derives from grand opera where such a character often carried a spear.

See BIT, SUPERNUMERARY.

special. An arrangement of stage lighting to define or emphasize a specific position on stage, for instance, a doorway or a couch, or a specific actor at an important moment in a play.

See LIGHTING PLOT.

specialty. A song or dance performed during a nonmusical play. It is presented in character and as part of the plot and is not intended to evoke applause or break into the flow of the play. It is performed not to the audience but to the cast members onstage. In Robert E. Sherwood's *Idiot's Delight,* Harry plays a Russian folk song on the piano in the hotel lounge. In James Thurber and Elliot Nugent's *The Male Animal,* Ellen and her former beau Joe dance to a record while her husband watches in dismay.

spectacle. The scenery, costumes, and special effects in a production. Aristotle called spectacle one of the six elements of drama, but he placed it last because, though spectacle may "gladden the soul," one may still read drama with profit rather than view it in a theatre.

See COSTUME, EXTRAVAGANZA, QUALITATIVE ELEMENTS OF DRAMA, SCENERY.

speeches. The lines said by an actor each time he or she speaks. Some actors count the number of speeches they have in a play to see how big their part is.

See LINES, SIDES.

spike. A mark on the stage floor that indicates the location of set furnishings.

spine. In the Stanislavsky method of actor's training, spine refers to the motivation that underlies a character's actions. Actors' Studio director Elia Kazan perceived the spine of Blanche's character in Tennessee Williams's *A Streetcar Named Desire* to be a search for a refuge from a brutal and hostile world.

See ACTORS' STUDIO, METHOD ACTING, MOTIVATION.

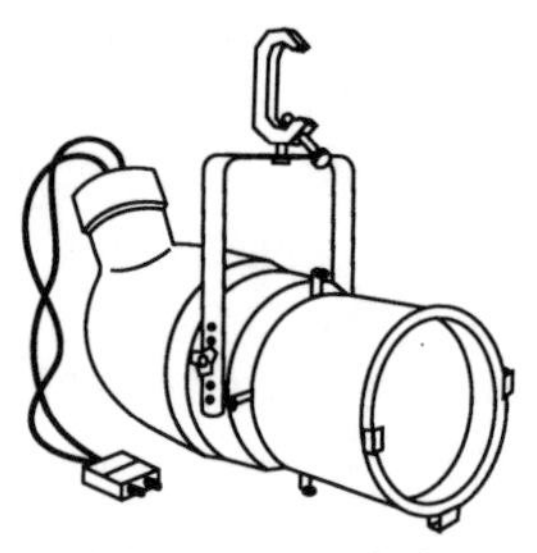

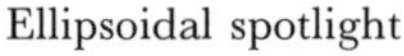

Ellipsoidal spotlight

Plano convex spotlight

spotlight. A light with a lens that throws an intense beam on a defined area. There are three types: The plano-convex has a lens that is flat on one side and convex on the other. Its beam is circular and sharp-edged. The Fresnel has a beam of greater intensity. The ellipsoidal spot has greater versatility than the other two because of its reflector. Sometimes the term *spotlight* is used mistakenly for any stage light.

The expression "in the spotlight" means to be the focus of attention.

See ERF, FRESNEL, LIGHTING PLOT, REFLECTOR.

SRO. An abbreviation for "standing room only." It means that all the seats for a performance have been sold and only reduced-priced tickets entitling one to stand at the back are left. Because of fire regulations, many theatres no longer permit standees, but the term is still used to signify a sold-out house.

stage. **1.** The area where the action of a play takes place. It may be an elevated platform or a clearing in the center of the audience.

See ARENA STAGE, CENTRAL STAGING, DECK, FOUND SPACE, OFF/ON STAGE, PROSCENIUM ARCH.

2. "To stage a play" means to rehearse and then perform it.

See REHEARSAL.

stage crew. The backstage technical crew responsible for running the show. In small theatre companies, often the same people build the set and handle the load-in, and then, during performances, change the scenery and handle the curtain.

See LOAD IN.

stage directions. Notes added to the script of a play, generally in italics or parentheses, that provide line readings, business, blocking, or directions for effects. Some playwrights provide a minimum of instructions, leaving the rest to the actors and director. G. B. Shaw, however, included very detailed stage directions. In *Arms and the Man,* Raina has a speech in which she merely says, "Ah!," but the stage directions tell her to wear a pretty nightgown, throw her cloak on the ottoman, dilate her eyes, and come eagerly to meet her mother. The stage directions are several times longer than the line they describe.

See BUSINESS, BLOCKING.

stage door. Located at the back or side of the theatre, it opens directly to the backstage area. Used by the actors and technical people, it is also the place to wait to ask for autographs. The expression "stage door Johnnies" came from the custom of men waiting with flowers and gifts for the women actors, especially those in the chorus in a musical.

stage left, right. Areas on the stage as seen from the actor's perspective, as opposed to "house left and right," which are from the audience's perspective.

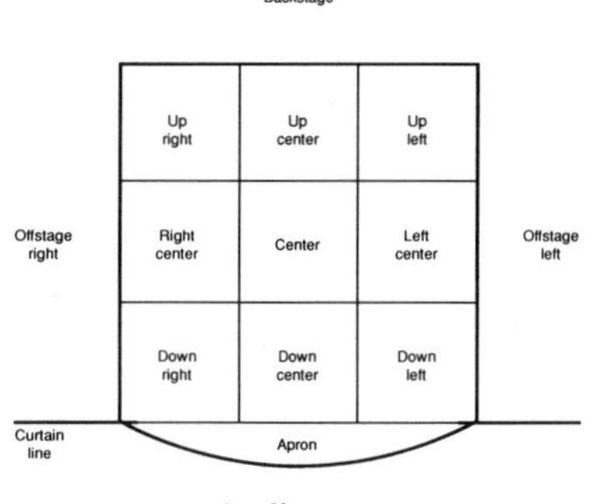

stage manager. The person responsible for overseeing all the backstage elements of a production: scheduling rehearsals, keeping the prompt book, rehearsing the understudies, supervising the prop man and wardrobe mistress, "calling the show" (signaling light, sound, and scenery change cues)—in effect, running the show from backstage.

See CUES.

star turn. The drawing of undue attention by an actor to himself or herself. A star turn may involve making faces, raising voice volume, crossing on another actor's lines, using unnecessary stage business, avoiding eye contact during an exchange of dialog, or not reacting properly to another actor's lines. Or it may involve playing a part on a level different from the others in the play, so that one stands out. The effect of a star turn is to pull an ensemble piece—such as Anton

Chekhov's *The Cherry Orchard,* Michael Frayn's *Noises Off,* or Robert Harling's *Steel Magnolias*—out of shape and ruin the balance of the play.

See ENSEMBLE PLAYING, FOCUS, HAM, UPSTAGE.

stasimon. In classical Greek drama, a choral ode sung and danced after the chorus has entered the orkestra area. In Euripides' *Iphigenia at Tauris,* the first stasimon has the chorus commenting on their arrival in Tauris. In the following stasima, they yearn to return home and they sing a hymn in praise of Apollo and the Delphic Oracle.

See CHORUS, ORKESTRA.

static characters. Those who remain the same throughout a play. Often, they are not major forces in the action but serve to fill out a cast. Or they may be static characters because of unrepentant evil or unswerving good. Things may happen to such characters without modifying their basic selves. Both Sheridan Whiteside in George Kaufman and Moss Hart's *The Man Who Came to Dinner* and Nicky Holroyd in John van Druten's *Bell, Book, and Candle* are at the center of the plot, but neither changes because of a basic uncaring, even selfish, amorality.

See DYNAMIC CHARACTER.

stations. In medieval drama, a series of stages representing settings of the play.

See MANSIONS.

stereotype. A character based on an assumption that all members of a particular race, creed, or class behave in the same way, so that a few devices—an accent, a religious article, jargon words—serve to delineate the character. McComber in Eugene O'Neill's *Ah, Wilderness!* is presented as the typical middle-class philistine, described as thin and dried up and dressed with a prim neatness.

See STOCK CHARACTERS.

stichomythia. Rapidly delivered dialog in which the characters speak alternate lines. The effect is that each character finishes the other's thoughts. Sophocles' *Electra* provides this example:

> ELECTRA: My mind was the same, my spirit weaker then.
> CHRYSOTHEMIS: Try to keep your spirit always constant.
> ELECTRA: This advice means you will not help me.
> CHRYSOTHEMIS: Your handiwork is likely to end badly.

Elizabethan playwrights used the same device, as seen in Shakespeare's *Richard III:*

> RICHARD: Say she shall be a high and mighty queen.
> QUEEN ELIZABETH: To vail the title as her mother doth.
> RICHARD: Say I will love her everlastingly.
> QUEEN ELIZABETH: But how long shall that title "ever" last?
> RICHARD: Sweetly in force unto her true live's end.
> QUEEN ELIZABETH: How long fairly shall her sweet life last?

In modern plays, stichomythia is used to heighten the suspense, as in plays by Samuel Beckett and Harold Pinter, or for comic effect, as in plays by Noel Coward and Tom Stoppard.

stock characters. Those who represent particular personality types or characteristics of human behavior. Stock characters appear throughout the history of theatre and are immediately recognizable. Greek new comedy and Roman comedy provided the original examples, such as the intriguer, the parasite, the skeptic, the virgin, the courtesan, the wily slave, and the braggart soldier. The commedia elaborated on these types in the characters of Harlequin the wily servant, Capitano the braggart soldier, Brighella the intriguer, Pantaloon the cuckold, and Olivetta the doxy. Modern stock characters include the wily servant Jeeves in P. G. Wodehouse's *Jeeves Takes Charge;* the airhead stewardess April in Stephen Sondheim's *Company;* the braggart soldier Carl-Magnus in Sondheim's *A Little Night Music;* the silly clubwoman Mrs. Stanley in George Kaufman and Moss Hart's *The Man Who Came to Dinner;* the unathletic brain Michael and the dumb athlete Wally in James Thurbur and Elliot Nugent's *The Male Animal.*

See STEREOTYPE, STOCK RESPONSE.

stock company. A resident company of actors presenting a series of plays for limited runs. In a true stock company, actors are hired to play certain parts: the tragedian or leading man who takes parts like Macbeth; the old man who does parts like Sir Peter Teazle in *School for Scandal;* the old woman who plays Juliet's nurse; the heavy father who plays villains; the heavy woman who takes parts like Lady Macbeth; the juvenile who plays Romeo; the ingenue who plays Juliet; the low comedian who takes the clown parts in the farces; the walking lady and gentleman who take small parts in comedies, often saying little more than a few lines while walking about the stage; the utility who plays minor roles in all types of plays; and the super who does walk-ons with no lines.

See INGENUE, JUVENILE, STOCK CHARACTERS, SUPERNUMERARY, SUMMER STOCK, UTILITY.

stock response. A conventional audience response to stock characters and situations: sympathy for the thwarted lovers, disgust at the intriguer, amusement at the wily servant.

See STOCK CHARACTERS.

stock situation. A situation recurring frequently in drama: mistaken identity, rags-to-riches, boy meets girl, return of the long-lost. Although stock situations evoke stock responses, they also provide the audience a sense of comfortable familiarity.

See STOCK CHARACTERS, STOCK RESPONSES.

straight man, woman. A character who feeds lines to the comic. Most comedy teams are composed of a straight man and comic. Margaret Dumont played straight woman to the Marx Brothers in several farces.

See FEED LINE, SECOND BANANA.

straw hat circuit. Summer theatres around the country that book equity companies of hit shows to play for a week or two.

See ACTORS' EQUITY.

street theatre. Performances in the open, usually by groups expressing the concerns of the area or general social problems.

See DIDACTIC, GUERRILLA THEATRE.

strike the set. To dismantle the setting of a play and reduce it to its basic elements at the end of a run. To strike the props is to remove them from the set until they are called for again. To strike a set in mid-performance is to clear away the setting to make room for the next act's scenery.

See PROPS, SCENERY, STAGE CREW.

strong curtain. An act that ends with a dramatically powerful line or action, used to arouse suspense or excitement for the act to follow.

See CURTAIN LINE.

strophe. In classical drama, the first division of a choral ode.
See ANTISTROPHE, CHORUS, CLASSICAL DRAMA.

structure. The overall framework or organization of the dramatic material. Plays are structured in scenes and acts. The pattern they follow is one of complication, rising action, climax, and resolution.
See PLOT.

studio theatre. A small theatre, usually seating no more than fifty, used for workshop productions, experimental plays, or rehearsal when the main stage is unavailable.
See MAIN STAGE, WORKSHOP.

style. The distinctive behavior, dress, and language of the characters. The style of a playwright is shown in the choices he or she makes: kinds of characters, time periods, settings, language, methods of characterization, use of symbols, and themes.
See CHARACTER, COSTUME, SET(TING), SYMBOL.

stylization. The shaping of dramatic material, settings, or costumes in a deliberately nonrealistic manner. For example, a stylization of trees might use triangles and circles on oblongs to suggest trees. The term also refers to an exaggerated manner of moving or speaking that calls attention to itself.
See SET DESIGNER.

subplot. A second plot subsidiary to the main one in a play. It may parallel and comment on the main plot, as does the below-stairs plot of Shakespeare's *Twelfth Night.* It may be just a side issue, as is the relationship between the vicar and Nigel in Simon Gray's *Hidden Laughter.* Or it may help the main plot along, as does Tom's striving to become a playwright in Arthur Pinero's *Trelawny of the "Wells."*

subtext. The thoughts, feelings, and reactions implied but never stated in the dialog of a play. The subtext may be supplied by the actors, by the director, or by both as they interpret the roles of the characters. To fully understand the play, the audience must be able to infer the subtext.

In this excerpt from Arthur Miller's *A View from the Bridge,* the subtext is enclosed within brackets following the dialog:

BEATRICE: . . . Was there ever any fella he liked for you? Even if it was a prince came here for you it wouldn't be no different. You know that don't you?
[Your uncle, my husband, is in love with you. That's why he won't let another man near you. You understand. Don't make me spell it out.]

CATHERINE: Yeah I guess so.
[I've seen what's happening, but I don't want to face it.]

BEATRICE: So what does that mean?
[This isn't easy for me. Help me out.]

CATHERINE: What?
[No, I'm not going to say it. I'm not going to help you with this.]

See CHOICES, INTERPRETATION, LINE READING.

summer stock. A stock company that operates only during the summer. Some of these are connected to universities and some, like the Williamstown (Mass.) Theatre Festival, are professional, using well-known actors, directors, and designers.
See STOCK COMPANY.

sunday. A knot used to tie several lines together to lift scenery.
See BAGLINE, CLEWING.

supernumerary. The actor who plays walk-on roles in the productions of a stock company. By extension, the term also refers to any actor who appears in a production but has no lines. In many Shakespeare plays, the *dramatis personae* included "lords, ladies, messengers, attendants, etc." These are the supernumeraries.

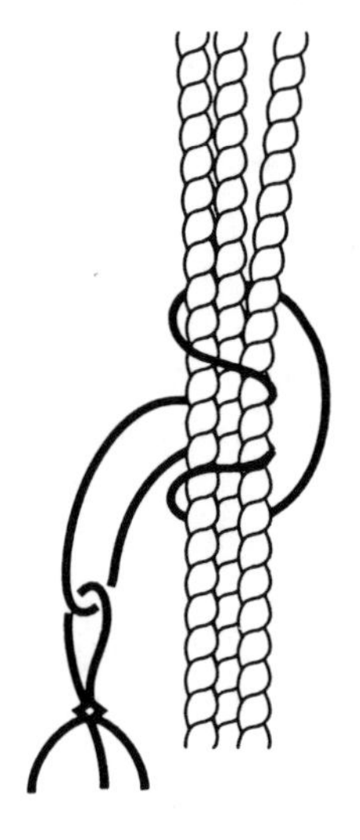

Sunday

superobjective. In the Stanislavsky method of actor's training, the character's long-range objective. In August Strindberg's *The Father,* Laura's superobjective is to control totally her daughter's upbringing.
See METHOD ACTING, SPINE.

surrealism. From the French *surréalisme,* coined in 1924, and meaning "above or beyond reality." It was a movement attacking formalism in the arts, the strict adherence to the guidelines for a form or genre. Surrealism was closely identified with Dadaism, but did not find much expression in the theatre, although Antonin Artaud, the French actor, producer, and writer, was associated with the movement at the beginning. Surrealism intended to transcend the accepted limitations of reality and bring dream material into literature and to synthesize the experiences of the unconscious and the conscious mind. Alfred Jarry's *Ubu Roi* is considered a forerunner of surrealistic drama. Jean Cocteau used surreal staging devices in *Orpheus* and *The Infernal Machine.*
See AVANT-GARDE, DADISM.

surround. Another name for *shroud.*

suspension of disbelief. The audience's willingness to accept the illusion and conventions of a theatre performance.
See AESTHETIC DISTANCE, CONVENTION, DRAMATIC TIME.

switchboard. The control panel for working the stage lighting.
See LIGHTING PLOT.

symbol. An object or event used in literature to expand on meaning. For example, when the sleepwalking Lady Macbeth tries to wash her hands, this ordinary action takes on a larger meaning. It becomes a symbol for her attempt to rid herself of guilt for what she has done. When Henrik Ibsen's Hedda Gabler shuns the bright sunlight in her interview with Miss Tesman, she says only that drawing the curtains will give a softer light, but the action takes on a deeper meaning. It is a symbol for Hedda's desire to keep hidden all her plans, motives, and schemes. In *The Glass Menagerie* by Tennessee Williams, the little glass unicorn of Laura's collection, in its fragility, its otherworldliness, its singularity, is a symbol for Laura herself. She, like the unicorn, is safe on a shelf, but when she is made to be part of the world she is hurt.
See ALLEGORY.

sympathy. An audience's identification with a character so that it trembles when he or she is afraid and rejoices when he or she is happy. A character is considered sympathetic when the audience takes an interest in and likes him or her. In Garson Kanin's *Born Yesterday,* the actor playing Billie must be sympathetic while the actor playing Harry should not be.

See HERO.

T

tableau. A grouping of silent, motionless actors representing an incident, often historical, and presenting an artistic spectacle. The tableau may conclude an act—as when actors freeze at the curtain line—or may be one in a series of tableaux that make up a pageant. In Stephen Sondheim's *Pacific Overtures,* the story unfolds in a series of striking tableaux to musical accompaniment.

See FREEZE, MASQUE, PAGEANT.

tails. Ropes dropped from a batten to hang scenery several feet below the batten instead of directly from it.

See BATTEN.

take, to do a. To react with facial expression or body language—often for humorous effect—to something seen or heard, for example, the open-mouthed, wide-eyed expression of a man who is dining out with his secretary and spots his wife at the next table.

See DOUBLE TAKE.

take direction. An actor's ability to understand and duplicate a line reading given by the director, or an actor's ability to respond accurately to suggestions about characterization given by the director.

See DIRECTOR, LINE READING.

take it down. An instruction from the director to an actor to reduce the energy, volume, or intensity in his or her line reading.

task play. A drama whose action revolves around some project to be carried out—cooking a meal, decorating a room, assembling a model airplane. In David Storey's *The Contractor,* a tent for a wedding reception is erected in the first act and dismantled in the last act.

See PRACTICAL SCENERY.

teaser. The horizontal drape at the top of a stage in a proscenium arch.

See PORTAL, PROSCENIUM ARCH, TORMENTOR.

techies. An affectionate nickname for technical crew members.

See STAGE CREW.

tech rehearsal. A rehearsal devoted to trying out the technical aspects of a production—scenery changes, costume changes, effects, sound cues, lighting, complicated props. The actors run through the play so that any technical problems can be dealt with.

See EFFECTS, LIGHTING PLOT, PROPS, RUN THROUGH, SCENERY, STAGE CREW.

tempo. The pace of a scene or play. The term also refers to the timing of an individual's performance within a scene or play. In reviewing Marc Camoletti's farce *Don't Dress for Dinner* at the Apollo in London, Ann McFerran noted that director Peter Farrago wisely used a tempo that gave the audience little time to keep up with the complications of the plot, much less think seriously about them.

See PACE.

tension. The state of anxiety induced in the audience by the threat of danger to a character in a play. Tension increases as the action rises to the climax and decreases as the action falls to the denouement. In Federico García Lorca's *The House of Bernarda Alba,* the tension builds as Bernarda decrees a prolonged period of cloistered mourning for herself and her five young daughters, and the audience knows the girls will not endure the situation for the eight years Bernarda has decreed.

See PLOT.

Terpsichore. One of the nine Olympian muses, Terpsichore is the patron of dancing. The art of dance is often called terpsichore.

See MELPOMENE, THALIA.

tetralogy. A group of four plays by the same playwright: a trilogy of related tragedies and a satyr play to provide comic relief and to commemorate Dionysus. Very little is known of the satyr plays, but one surviving trilogy is Aeschylus' *Orestia,* composed of *Agamemnon, Libation Bearers,* and *The Eumenides.* In classical Greece, yearly festivals were held at Athens where each playwright offered a tetralogy and the winner was awarded a laurel wreath.

See DIONYSUS, SATYR PLAY, TRAGEDY, TRILOGY.

Thalia. One of the nine muses, Thalia was the patron of comedy.

See MELPOMENE, TERPSICHORE.

theatre. The total artistic experience of drama, either by the presenter ("I work in the theatre") or by the audience ("I love the theatre"). Also, a building where plays are presented. Also, a movement or a style of presentation in the evolution of the theatre.

See ABSURD, THEATRE OF THE; BOULEVARD DRAMA; BOURGEOIS DRAMA; CLASSICAL DRAMA; COMEDY OF HUMORS; COMEDY OF MANNERS; COMMEDIA DELL'ARTE; CRUELTY, THEATRE OF; DADAISM; DOMESTIC TRAGEDY; EPIC THEATRE; FRINGE THEATRE; GUERRILLA THEATRE; HEROIC DRAMA; HOUSE MANAGER; JACOBEAN REVENGE TRAGEDY; KABUKI; LUNCHTIME THEATRE; MEDIEVAL DRAMA; MELODRAMA; MUSICAL THEATRE; NAUTICAL DRAMA; NEOCLASSICISM; NOH; OFF BROADWAY; PLANT; VAUDEVILLE.

theatre games. A type of improvisation carefully structured by the director to achieve a specific objective: break down inhibitions, establish trust, determine relationships within a play. Many games use devices borrowed from psychology. Although the terms *improvisation* and *theatre games* are often used interchangeably, it's helpful to distinguish between them. Theatre games have more careful structure and a stated purpose; improvisation may include anything from covering for a missed line in performance to actors asking the audience for first lines and premises and then making up a skit to fit them.

See AD-LIB, IMPROVISATION.

theatre-in-the-round. A form of play presentation in which the audience surrounds the acting area.

See ARENA STAGE.

theatricalism. A reaction against the realism of the early 1900s. Theatricalism asserted that theatre is not life but merely carefully selected and arranged details of the playwright's, director's, or actor's vision of life. Epic theatre, with its insistence to audience members that they are watching a play, is a kind of theatricalism, as is the device of the play-within-a-play. Thornton Wilder, Edward Albee, Jack Gelber, Arthur Kopit, and Max Frisch use all aspects of theatre in order to define the play as a staged work, not a slice of real life.

See EPIC THEATRE, NATURALISM, REALISM, SLICE OF LIFE.

theatron. The place where the audience sat in classical Greek theatre. It was a hollowed-out hillside, in the open air, roughly semicircular, with a capacity of as many as 17,000 people (Theatre of Dionysus at Athens).

See ORKESTRA, PROSKENIUM, SKENE.

theme. What the play means as opposed to what happens (the plot). Sometimes the theme is clearly stated in the title: *Butterflies Are Free* (Leonard Gershe), *The Play's the Thing* (Ferenc Molnár), *All for Love* (John Dryden). It may be stated by a character acting as the playwright's voice. In George Kelly's *Craig's Wife,* the aunt tells Mrs. Craig that people who live to themselves are often left to themselves. Or it may be that the theme is less obvious and emerges only after some study or thought. Peter Shaffer's *Equus* seems to say that the power to make life normal may also make it pointless.

See DIDACTIC, THOUGHT.

theologeion. In classical Greek theatre, a platform on the roof of the *skene* where actors playing gods or heroes make pronouncements, such as those of Thetis in Euripides' *Andromache* and Iris in his *Mad Heracles.*

See DEUX EX MACHINA, SKENE.

thesis play. One that offers a specific solution for a social problem.

See PROBLEM PLAY.

Thespis. A Greek poet (550–500 B.C.) usually considered the founder of drama because he was the first one to use an actor in addition to the chorus in his plays. Some theatre historians believe that Thespis was that first actor. Although none of his plays remain, some titles are known: *Phorbus, The Priests, The Youths,* and *Pentheus.*
See CHORUS, PROTAGONIST.

thought. The second of what Aristotle considered the six qualitative elements of drama. *Thought* refers to the themes, arguments, and overall meaning of a play. It is present in even the most trivial of plays since a playwright cannot help expressing some ideas in the course of the action.
See THEME.

through-sung. A term coined by composer Andrew Lloyd Webber to describe his musical plays *(Aspects of Love, Cats, Phantom of the Opera, Evita)* that have no dialog, but use lyrics to carry forward the plot.
See BOOK, LYRICS.

thrust stage. A low platform stage surrounded on three sides by the audience. It has the advantage of retaining one side for drops, scenery, entrances, and exits and yet providing a sense of intimacy with the audience. Two stages of this type are the Guthrie in Minneapolis and the Shakespeare Memorial Theatre in Stratford, Ontario, Canada.
See APRON, ARENA STAGE.

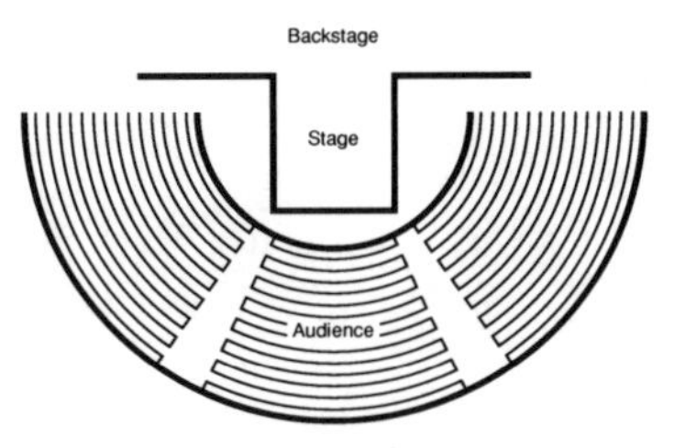

Thrust stage

thunder sheet. An offstage sound effect that uses a piece of heavy sheet metal, about six feet by two, clasped securely between two battens at the top and having a handle or tab at the bottom. The handle is grasped and the sheet shaken to produce the sound of a roll of thunder.
See EFFECTS.

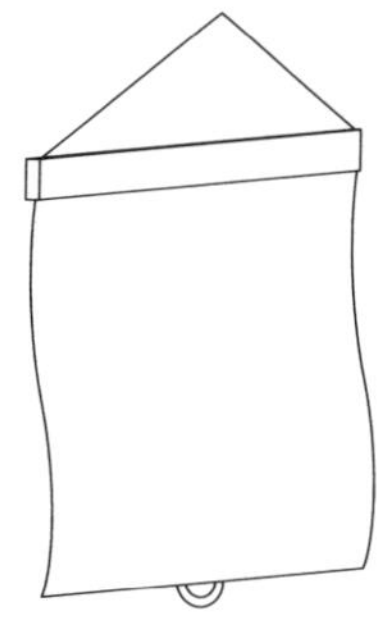
Thunder sheet

timing. This term includes the setting of cues for effects, stage business, and lighting for maximum effectiveness; synchronization of two or more things that must happen simultaneously; and selection of the pace at which lines will be delivered or the entire play performed. Poor timing of a comic line can kill the expected laugh, and poor timing of a serious line can provoke an unwanted laugh.

See PACE, TEMPO.

tirade. In French neoclassical theatre, an impassioned speech delivered in the manner of an operatic aria, with the body almost rigid and all energy going to the voice. The speech is long and formal, and develops a rhetorical argument. In Molière's *Tartuffe,* Orgon's fervent defense of Tartuffe to his brother-in-law Cleante is a tirade.

See NEOCLASSICAL.

tone. The playwright's attitude toward his or her material. The material itself does not dictate tone since absurdist comedy often deals with serious matters. The tone may be nostalgic, as in Brian Friel's Olivier Award–winning *Dancing at Lughnasa;* serious, as in Barbara Lebow's *Shayna Maidel;* playful, as in Joseph Kesselring's *Arsenic and Old Lace;* or ironic, as in Keith Hurt's adaptation of Mikhail Bulgakov's *Black Snow.*

Tony Awards. Nickname for the Antoinette Perry Awards given annually for the best theatre work on Broadway.

See ANTOINETTE PERRY AWARDS, BROADWAY.

top hat. A short metal cylinder used to control a light beam.

See FUNNEL.

tormentor. The vertical drape that masks the wings at each side of a proscenium arch. A tormentor may be a heavy wooden framework covered with rough painted canvas that is then covered with a softer ornamental fabric, or, as is the case in many school auditoriums, simply the ornamental drapery fabric. The term is derived from the Latin *tortuo,* meaning "twist."

See MASK, PROSCENIUM ARCH, RETURN, TEASER, WINGS.

tragedy. A term, perhaps derived from the Greek *tragoedia,* that refers to serious plays that end unhappily. In its earliest known form, tragedy was a Greek choral ode sung at the festival of Dionysus. It evolved into the classical drama of Sophocles, Aeschylus, and Euripides. Roman drama based most of its material on Greek originals, and the tragedies of Renaissance Italy also looked to Greek models. The purpose of tragedy, according to Aristotle, is to arouse in the audience feelings of pity and fear that are then purged at the play's conclusion.

English Renaissance tragedies did not always adhere to the classical unities or to the concept of a tragic hero falling because of a tragic flaw, but French neoclassical tragedy did favor a return to Greek models.

Twentieth-century tragic plays are more likely to deal with domestic or social concerns. There is even a mixture of forms called tragicomedy.

See ANTIHERO, BOURGEOIS DRAMA, CLASSICAL DRAMA, CONTAMINATION, DIONYSIAN, HERO, HEROIC DRAMA, JACOBEAN REVENGE TRAGEDY, KATHARSIS, MELODRAMA, PATHOS, PITY AND FEAR, ROMAN DRAMA, TRAGIC FLAW, TRAGIC HERO, TRAGOEDIA.

tragic flaw. The defect in the tragic hero that leads to his or her fall.

See HAMARTIA, HYBRIS, TRAGIC HERO.

tragic hero. The central figure in a tragedy. Aristotle described the tragic hero as a man who passes from happiness to misery, not as a result of vice or baseness but because of a flaw of character and error in judgment. He must not be a perfectly virtuous and just man, but one of basically good character, and he must belong to a distinguished family so that the fall will be all the greater. He must arouse pity and fear in the audience as they vicariously share his sufferings. Oedipus of Sophocles' *Oedipus Rex* serves as an example: he passes from triumph to exile, not because he has been a bad husband or father or ruler, but because years before in youthful impetuosity he caused the death of a man and married his widow. The information that the man was his father and the widow his mother was withheld from Oedipus until a plague devastated his city and only his punishment would appease the gods.

In modern drama, the tragic hero is more likely to be a representative common man or woman whose fall does not have the widespread repercussion of that of the classical hero. Examples are William Inge's depressed housewife in *Come Back, Little Sheba,* Arthur Miller's traveling salesman in *Death of a Salesman,* and Elmer Rice's clerk in *The Adding Machine.*

See ANTIHERO, HERO, TRAGEDY, TRAGIC FLAW.

tragoedia. Greek, meaning "goat song," the *dithyramb* or hymn to Dionysus that is considered the origin of drama.

See CLASSICAL DRAMA, DIONYSIAN, DITHYRAMB, KOMOS.

trap. An opening in the floor of the stage used for appearance and disappearance effects.

See DISAPPEARANCE TRAP.

trilogy. A sequence of three plays on the same theme or sharing the same characters, but each complete in itself. The only surviving Greek trilogy is Aeschylus' *Orestia.* Other trilogies are Eugene O'Neill's reworking of the *Orestia, Mourning Becomes Electra,* and, recently, Alan Ayckbourn's *The Norman Conquests.*

See TETRALOGY.

tritagonist. An actor in Greek drama, third after the protagonist and deuteragonist, who performed minor roles—for example, the Priest and the Herdsman in *Oedipus Rex.*

See PROTAGONIST, DEUTERAGONIST.

tryouts. Auditions. Also, performances of a show before it opens on Broadway. New Haven, Conn.; Boston; and Philadelphia were favorite places for such tryouts, but recent plays have had preview runs on Broadway, often with reduced-price tickets, before their premieres. Sometimes plays are workshopped for long periods in one location or around the country before their premieres.

See AUDITION, PREMIERE, WORKSHOP PRODUCTION.

turning point. The moment in a play when events can go either way; the moment of decision; the crisis.

See CLIMAX, CRISIS, DENOUEMENT, PLOT.

typecasting. The casting of roles in a play by choosing actors who most closely resemble the physical and personality descriptions of the characters. Typecasting is mostly an outgrowth of realism, but it is also a quick way of assembling a cast. Actors who find themselves typecast may want to work in different kinds of parts or as guest artists with an academic theatre just to show what else they can do.

See ACADEMIC THEATRE, EQUITY WAIVER HOUSE, SHOWCASE.

understudy. One who is prepared to take over an important role should the actor playing the role miss a performance. Often, the understudy also has a small role in the play. The understudy must be able to keep the quality of the play unchanged when he or she steps into the part. An announcement on a board in the lobby, on a slip of paper in the program, and, sometimes, over a loudspeaker tells the audience that an understudy will act in a performance. Shirley MacLaine was understudy to Carol Haney in George Abbott's *The Pajama Game.*

See MATINEE.

unities. Three principles of dramatic structure required in a play—unity of time, action, and place. Unity of time means the play takes place in a period not to exceed twenty-four hours. Unity of place calls for one unchanged scene throughout the play. In Greek drama, the chorus narrated offstage events and messengers brought news from other places. Unity of action requires one plot with no subplots. Only the last unity was strictly adhered to by Greek tragedians. Roman tragedy, as seen in the works of Seneca, adhered to the first two, but not the third. Although Aristotle described all three, he insisted on only unity of action.

See CLASSICAL DRAMA.

unit set. An arrangement of scenery in which some or all of the pieces can be used in different combinations for different scenes. It may be a permanent frame that stands throughout the play with the individual flats put in and taken out as needed. Or the pieces for one scene may simply be reassembled for the next. For example, an arrangement of free-standing shrubbery might be used in groupings of two, three, or four at different points in the play. Thus, a few simple pieces and some lighting changes can represent all the scenes in a play. This technique is widely used in performing Shakespeare's plays so that one short scene flows quickly and easily into the next.

See DETAIL SCENERY, FLAT, SET.

universality. The quality of some literature, dealing with basic human emotions and situations common to all people, that is faithful to the truths of human psychology, motivation, and behavior. Critics have found universality in the plays of Shakespeare whereas once-popular plays like James Rado and Gerome Ragni's *Hair* seem dated and of interest mainly as sociological curiosities.

See THEME.

upstage. The area of the stage farthest away from the audience. Stages were once raked (slanted upward toward the back) so that area was indeed "up."

upstaging. Standing upstage of another actor, forcing him or her to face away from the audience in order to exchange dialog. In the time of the raked stage, such action gave the first actor more of the audience's attention. Now the term refers to using any sort of business to take attention away from another actor.

See BUSINESS, GESTURE, MUGGING, STAR TURN.

utility. In a stock company, the actor who plays minor roles in all types of plays for a small salary. Called so because he or she is an all-purpose player in the company.

See BIT, STOCK COMPANY.

vagabond theatre. A term used by playwright and theatre historian Ronald Harwood to describe the troupes of players who, after the fall of Rome, kept theatre alive by traveling the countryside performing wherever they could for whatever pay—food or lodging mostly—they could get. Most likely, these were family groups whose juggling, acrobatics, singing, dancing, and comic routines were passed down from generation to generation, culminating centuries later in the *commedia dell'arte.*

See COMMEDIA DELL'ARTE, STOCK CHARACTERS.

Variety. The "show business Bible." A weekly journal that details the news of show business. (A daily issue deals mainly with film and television.) It includes gossip, play reviews, theatre schedules, and celebrity obituaries as well as feature articles and interviews.

vaudeville. A counterpart of the English music hall, vaudeville is light entertainment consisting of ten to fifteen individual acts—singing, dancing, acrobatics, comic skits and monologs, animal performers, magic—all unrelated in one show. Famous acts included (Joseph) Weber and (Lew) Fields and the Foy Family (Eddie Foy and his seven children). Even serious stage actors like Mrs. Patrick Campbell and Sarah Bernhardt appeared on vaudeville programs in dramatic sketches. At one time, playing the Palace Theatre in New York City, a vaudeville house, was synonymous with reaching the top in show business. The introduction of sound motion pictures and radio hastened the demise of vaudeville.

See MUSIC HALL.

verisimilitude. Creating the impression of reality in the mind of the audience so that it will accept the characters and actions as true to life. Aristotle believed that the audience must be convinced of the logic of the fiction it sees in the drama.

See MOTIVATION.

verse drama. A play written in poetic form—blank verse, for example, or heroic couplets. Twentieth-century writers of verse drama include Christopher Fry *(The Lady's Not for Burning),* Maxwell Anderson *(Winterset),* and T. S. Eliot *(Murder in the Cathedral).*

See ALEXANDRINE, COUPLET, HEROIC COUPLET, HEROIC DRAMA.

Vice. In the morality play, Vice was the stock figure of wickedness. Usually more buffoon than serious threat, he fought Good Deeds and was vanquished to Hell. Often, he was crowned with ass's ears and played second to the devil in the mock battle of wits that was a staple of morality plays. Vice appears in such plays as *Mankind* and *The Castle of Perseverance,* and is seen as late as 1560 in *The Lamentable Tragedy, Mixed Full of Mirth, Containing the Life of Cambises, King of Persia.*

See INTERLUDE, MORALITY PLAY.

villain. The evil character who opposes the hero or heroine. Well-known villains are Don John in Shakespeare's *Much Ado About Nothing,* Lawyer Cribbs in P. T. Barnum's *The Drunkard,* Professor Moriarity in William Gillette's *Sherlock Holmes,* and Fistula in Vaclav Havel's *Temptation.*

See ANTAGONIST, HEAVY.

voice projection. Control of loudness so that even those in the last row can hear and understand every word of dialog in the play. Projection requires good breathing techniques to produce a loud, firm voice; a relaxed and open throat so that the voice is not pinched but, rather, resonates; and crisp enunciation so that the words are spoken distinctly.

wagon. A rolling cart used for moving scenery. Designer Cleon Throckmorton used this device in a production of Eugene O'Neill's *Beyond the Horizon.* In a previous production of the play, the last scene had to be omitted because the scene change took too long. Throckmorton used the wagons to accomplish the change in less than a minute.

See BOAT TRUCK, JACKKNIFE.

wardrobe mistress. The technical staff member responsible for the care of the costumes for a show. If stars have individual dressing rooms and dressers, their costumes may be kept there, but the costumes for the rest of the cast are under the direct supervision of the wardrobe mistress, who must check for tears and soiling after each performance. The wardrobe mistress also assists in quick change, especially any that have to be made just offstage.

See COSTUME, COSTUME SHOP.

wash. A soft, single-color light that bathes the set. A favorite choice is a blue wash over the entire set. The wash is convenient when the theatre has no front curtain. The wash can be used before the play begins. Then, after the house lights are dimmed, the lighting plot can be put into effect without having been spoiled by a premature appearance.

See LIGHTING PLOT.

well-made play. A pattern of tight and logical play construction that began with French playwright Eugène Scribe (1791–1861), who called it *pièce bien faite.* It uses such dramatic devices as a secret withheld until the climax; a reversal of fortune for the hero; mounting suspense depending on mislaid papers; misidentified characters; a battle of wits between hero and villain; an obligatory scene in which the secret is revealed; and a logical denouement that accounts for all the threads of the plot. The plays of Scribe and his follower Victorien Sardou influenced British playwrights Arthur Pinero, Arthur Henry Jones, Somerset Maugham, Oscar Wilde, and Terence Rattigan.

See COMEDY OF MANNERS, CONVENTIONS, HERO, OBLIGATORY SCENE, VILLAIN.

West End. The London equivalent of New York City's theatre district. Some of the theatres located there are the Comedy, the Haymarket, the Lyric, the Apollo, and the Prince of Wales.

See BROADWAY.

Whitehall farce. Plays in the tradition of the old Aldwych farces. In 1950, Brian Rix began staging a series of popular farces by Ray Cooney, John Chapman, and Tony Hilton. The pace was fast; the structure, traditional farce; and the subject matter, topical. For example, Ray Cooney's *Chase Me Comrade* (1964) alluded to the defection from Russia of ballet star Rudolf Nureyev.

See ALDWYCH FARCE, FARCE.

wild. The jog, or hinged, portion of a setting that is free to move.

See FLAT, JOG, SCENERY.

wind machine. An offstage mechanism, either electrical or hand driven, that creates a breeze on the set to blow leaves, curtains, costumes, and so forth.

See EFFECTS.

wing. A canvas-covered flat, painted black or to match the set, and mounted at the side of a backdrop to mask the sides of the set. Also refers to a single flat.

See FLAT, MASK.

wings. The area immediately offstage left and right where actors stand to await their cues. The term originated from the practice of actors standing behind the wing pieces of a drop-and-wing set before they went onstage. That area is closed off by a box set, but the name remains.

See BOX SET, DROP.

word play. Verbal fencing, punning, or mock bickering. Examples include that between Beatrice and Benedick in Shakespeare's *Much Ado About Nothing,* or Oscar and Felix in Neil Simon's *The Odd Couple.* In William Congreve's *The Way of the World,* Mirabell and Millamant conduct their courtship through the word play of their mock bickering:

MILLAMANT: One no more owes one's beauty to a lover than one's wit to an echo; they can but reflect what we look and say—vain empty things if we are silent or unseen, and want a being.

MIRABELL: Yet, to those two vain empty things you owe two of the greatest pleasures of your life.

MILLAMANT: How so?

MIRABELL: To your lover you owe the pleasure of hearing yourselves praised, and to an echo the pleasure of hearing yourselves talk.

workshop. A place for putting together and polishing a production. Also, a place where one can receive instruction and practice in directing, acting, and stagecraft.

"To workshop" a play means to prepare it for performance and then present it while continuing to change, adjust, and polish it. Generally, the play is not subject to professional review during this time.

workshop production. A work in progress. The playwright and director, and sometimes the actors as well, continue to work on a play as they present it to a paying or nonpaying preview audience. Things may be added or whole sections deleted as they go along. Stephen Sondheim and James Lapine workshopped *Into the Woods* at the Old Globe Theatre in San Diego, Calif., before bringing it to Broadway. In the process they cut a Three Little Pigs and a Rumplestiltskin sequence. A Daly City, Calif., workshop for young Filipino-Americans yielded scenes chronicling the experiences of several Filipino families living in

San Francisco. A team of seven writers then worked with director Chris B. Millado to shape the material into *Kin,* a two-hour production mounted by the Teatro ng Tanan at the Fort Mason (Calif.) Cowell Theatre.

The term is also used in academic theatre to designate productions other than those on the mainstage.

See MAINSTAGE PRODUCTION.

Z

zany. Also *zanni.* At first, the proper name of a servant-clown character of the commedia; later, any clown, especially a clown's comic assistant and the butt of his jokes. Some theatre historians believe the name *zani* was first given to the masks worn by Harlequin and Brighella because they were descendants of the sannio, or clown figures, of the fabula atellana. The term is also used for the toy clown's head on a stick, made to look like the jester who carries it.

See COMMEDIA DELL'ARTE, CLOWN CHARACTER, FABULA ATELLANA, HARLEQUIN.